Democracy and Urban Governance in India

Published in association with
Observer Research Foundation
New Delhi

Observer Research Foundation (ORF) is a public policy think-tank that aims to influence formulation of policies for building a strong and prosperous India. The ORF pursues these goals by providing informed and productive inputs, in-depth research and stimulating discussion. The Foundation is supported in its mission by a cross-section of India's leading public figures, academics and business leaders.

ABOUT THE AUTHOR

Rumi Aijaz is Senior Fellow at the Observer Research Foundation in New Delhi, India. He is also an associate member of the Institute of Town Planners, India. He received his doctoral degree in Urban Governance from the School of Planning and Architecture in New Delhi, and has been a post-doctoral Visiting Fellow at the London School of Economics and Political Science.

His research interests are primarily in the areas of urbanisation, urban development, urban and regional planning, urban infrastructure and services, urban management and governance, geography and social development. Dr. Aijaz has written on some of these topics and his articles have been published in leading journals, such as *Habitat International, Journal of Asian and African Studies, Journal of the Institute of Town Planners, India, Urban India* and *Seminar*.

Democracy and Urban Governance in India

RUMI AIJAZ

ACADEMIC FOUNDATION
NEW DELHI

www.academicfoundation.com

First published in 2012
by

ACADEMIC FOUNDATION
4772-73 / 23 Bharat Ram Road, (23 Ansari Road),
Darya Ganj, New Delhi - 110 002 (India).
Phones : 23245001 / 02 / 03 / 04.
Fax : +91-11-23245005.
E-mail : books@academicfoundation.com
www.academicfoundation.com

in association with the
Observer Research Foundation, New Delhi

Cataloging in Publication Data--DK
Courtesy: D.K. Agencies (P) Ltd. <docinfo@dkagencies.com>

Aijaz, Rumi.
Democracy and urban governance in India / Rumi Aijaz.
p. cm.
ISBN 13: 9788171889082
ISBN 10: 8171889085

1. Municipal government--India. 2. Democracy--India. I. Title.

DDC 352.160954 23

Typeset by Italics India, New Delhi.
Printed and bound in India.

Contents

List of Tables, Figures, Boxes and Annexures

Tables

Figures

Boxes

Annexures

Abbreviations

AIILSG	All India Institute of Local Self-Government
ARV	Annual Rental Value
ADB	Asian Development Bank
CESC	Calcutta Electricity Supply Corporation
CGG	Centre for Good Governance
CSB	Citizen Service Bureau
CDP	City Development Plan
CMA	City Managers' Association
C&AG	Comptroller and Auditor General
CAA	Constitution (74th Amendment) Act
CREF	Credit Rating Enhancement Fund
CRISIL	Credit Rating Information Services of India Limited
DDA	Delhi Development Authority
DJB	Delhi Jal Board
DMRC	Delhi Metro Rail Corporation
DFID	Department for International Development
DIT	Department of Information Technology
DPR	Detailed Project Report
DPC	District Planning Committee
ECIL	Electronics Corporation of India Limited
GoI	Government of India
GoR	Government of Rajasthan
GoU	Government of Uttarakhand

GoUP	Government of Uttar Pradesh
HUDCO	Housing and Urban Development Corporation
IIPA	Indian Institute of Public Administration
INR	Indian Rupee
ICICI	Industrial Credit and Investment Corporation of India
ICT	Information and Communication Technology
IT	Information Technology
IDFC	Infrastructure Development Finance Company
IL&FS	Infrastructure Leasing and Financial Services
ICMA	International City/County Management Association
JBIC	Japan Bank for International Cooperation
JNNURM	Jawaharlal Nehru National Urban Renewal Mission
KEIP	Kolkata Environmental Improvement Project
KMC	Kolkata Municipal Corporation
LG	Lieutenant Governor
LIC	Life Insurance Corporation
LOGOTRI	Local Government Training and Research Institutes
MLA	Member of Legislative Assembly
MPLADS	Member of Parliament Local Area Development Scheme
MPC	Metropolitan Planning Committee
MoC&IT	Ministry of Communications and Information Technology
MoUD	Ministry of Urban Development
MoUD&PA	Ministry of Urban Development and Poverty Alleviation
MML	Model Municipal Law
MCD	Municipal Corporation of Delhi
NCT	National Capital Territory of Delhi
NeGP	National e-Governance Plan

NMMP	National Mission Mode Project
NMAM	National Municipal Accounts Manual
NSDP	National Slum Development Programme
NGO	Non-government Organisation
NDPL	North Delhi Power Limited
FPDF	Pooled Finance Development Fund
PPP	Public-Private Partnership
PFDS	Pooled Finance Development Scheme
PTI	Press Trust of India
RCUES	Regional Centre for Urban and Environmental Studies
SFC	State Finance Commission
SLNA	State-level Nodal Agency
SPFE	State Pooled Finance Entity
TCS	Tata Consultancy Services
TOI	Times of India
UT	Union Territory
UNCHS	United Nations Centre for Human Settlements
UNDP	United Nations Development Programme
UNESCAP	United Nations Economic and Social Commission for Asia and the Pacific
USAID	United States Agency for International Development
USAEP	United States-Asia Environmental Partnership
UA	Urban Agglomeration
ULB	Urban Local Body
ULGI	Urban Local Government Institution
UAoA	Uttarakhand Academy of Administration
VMC	Vijayawada Municipal Corporation

Foreword

The pace at which urbanisation has of late been occurring is striking. In 1950, there were 86 cities in the world with a population over one million; today there are 400, and by 2015, there will be at least 550. Cities, indeed, have absorbed nearly two-thirds of the global population explosion since 1950 and are currently growing by a million babies and migrants each week. The present urban population is larger than the total population of the world in 1960. The global countryside, meanwhile, has reached its maximum population (3.2 billion) and will begin to shrink after 2020. As a result, cities will account for all future world population growth, which is expected to peak at about 10 billion in 2050.

India is no exception to the general trend of a fast increase in the population of cities and the intractable complexity of the problems that it is causing. Although the percentage of urban population to the total population has not risen sharply—it has moved from about 14 per cent in 1951 to about 28 per cent at present—yet in sheer numbers it has shown a very high increase. Presently, the urban population of India is about 300 million which exceeds the total population of India at the time of Independence. During the last 50 years, India has, on an average, been adding about five to six million people to its towns and cities. There are already five mega-cities (five million plus), 31 micro-cities (one million plus) and about 350 large towns, besides 4,800 small and medium size urban settlements. The Economic and Social Commission for Asia and the Pacific (ESCAP) estimates that between 1990 and 2020, India would add 418 million people to its urban population.

To house this massive urban population and to meet its civic needs and its social and cultural aspirations and also to keep its environment healthy is going to present to the human race one of the gravest challenges that it has ever faced. The UN Commission on Human Settlements has rightly underlined:

> It is in the cities, towns and hamlets of the new urban world that the majority of us will live and work in the new century where most of the pollution will be generated and natural resources, consumed, where political and social conditions are likely to boil over in conflict and where, ultimately, the roots of global security—true human security—will lie.

Clearly, it is of utmost importance that all our institutions of urban governance, especially municipal corporations, municipal councils and *nagar panchayats*, are substantially strengthened and their administrative, financial and technological capacities upgraded. Of late, the Government of India has moved in the right direction and taken a number of policy initiatives. These initiatives have been concretised and incorporated in the country's Five-Year Plans.

But the basic issue remains. It is one of implementation. Whether the new practices would yield intended results or not would depend upon the manner in which the plans and programmes are executed. It is, therefore, crucial that pace and pattern of implementation are periodically and independently assessed and correctives applied wherever deficiencies are found.

Rumi Aijaz has picked up, for his study, four practices emanating from the aforesaid policy initiatives. These pertain to revision of municipal laws, capacity-building for municipal functionaries, e-governance and strengthening of municipal finances. Each policy/practice has been subjected to separate examination. His approach is sound and his conclusions balanced. Whereas he has noted the substantial headway made in certain respects, he has not hesitated to underscore the negative elements that still persist in other spheres.

I have no doubt that Aijaz's study/research work would be useful not only to policymakers and implementers but also to the students and teachers of urban affairs.

Jagmohan

Former Governor of J&K and
Former Union Minister of Communication,
Urban Development, Poverty Alleviation,
Tourism and Culture.

Acknowledgements

During the conduct of this study, the author met numerous knowledgeable persons who spared their valuable time to share their experiences on local governance and provided important data and information. Their names along with institutional affiliation are given below.

Nainital Municipal Council: Ms. Sarita Arya [Chairperson], Mr. K.N. Painuly [Executive Officer], Mr. S.C. Choudhari [Accountant], Mr. Devendra Joshi [Junior Engineer], Mr. Mahesh Gururani [Meeting Clerk], Mr. Rajinder Pargaien [Councillor, Ward No. 1], Mr. Deepak Kumar [Councillor, Ward No. 3].

Uttarakhand Academy of Administration, Nainital: Mr. D.S. Dhapola [Project Director, Urban Affairs Unit], Mr. Dinesh Mahtolia [Senior Project Manager].

Municipal Corporation of Delhi (MCD): Mr. S.K. Rastogi [Additional District Commissioner, Information Technology Department], Mr. Amit Prasad [Assessor and Joint Collector, Property Tax Department], Mr. Arun Kumar [Executive Engineer (Civil)], Mr. Gopal Khanna [Superintendent, Factory and Licensing Department], Mr. Amlendu Mukherjee [Electronics Corporation of India Limited], Ms. Savita Gupta [Councillor, Ward No. 57–Paschim Vihar (South), West Zone], Mr. Vikas Taank [Councillor, Ward No. 78–Majnu ka Tila, Civil Lines Zone], Ms. Veena Abrol [Councillor, Ward No. 155–Lajpat Nagar I, Central Zone], Dr. Annapurna Mishra [Councillor, Ward No. 272–Sonia Vihar, Shahdara North Zone].

Kolkata Municipal Corporation: Shri Alapan Bandyopadhyay [Municipal Commissioner], Shri Debatosh Dasgupta [Comptroller of Municipal Finance and Accounts (CMFA)], Shri Swapan Mukherjee [Additional CMFA (Accounts)], Shri Ayan Dutta Gupta [Deputy Chief Accountant], Shri Tapan Kar [Municipal Accountant].

The author has benefitted immensely from the advice and suggestions given by Mr. Lojy Thomas [Regional Director, All India Institute of Local Self-Government, New Delhi], and Dr. P. Jayapal [Executive Director (Projects), Social Housing/Core Infrastructure, HUDCO, New Delhi].

Mr. Jagmohan [Former Governor of Jammu and Kashmir and Former Union Minister of Communication, Urban Development, Poverty Alleviation, Tourism and Culture] kindly agreed to write the foreword, to whom the author is indebted.

The author is grateful to (Late) Shri R.K. Mishra [Founder and Former Chairman of the Observer Research Foundation], and Prof. Rakesh Basant [faculty at Indian Institute of Management, Ahmedabad, also associated with ORF]. They recognised the necessity and usefulness of promoting policy research on urbanisation and related issues at ORF. This study was completed under the supervision and guidance of Prof. Rakesh Basant.

Valuable advice on the final manuscript was received from Mr. Surendra Singh [Former Cabinet Secretary], which helped in improving its quality.

At ORF, complete encouragement and support was received from Mr. M. Rasgotra, Mr. Surendra Singh, Mr. Sunjoy Joshi, Mr. Baljit Kapoor, Ms. Anshu John, Mr. Samir Saran and Mr. Vidyadharan.

Ms. Neha Arora [affiliated with ORF as Junior Fellow in 2008] assisted in the collection and compilation of information on e-Governance initiatives of the MCD. Mr. Manish Vaid [Research Assistant, ORF] offered help in the collection of latest data and information on various urban governance practices from secondary sources.

The author is also thankful to the ORF administration and IT staff, who have helped in various ways.

1 Introduction

Urban areas in India offer numerous opportunities of livelihood and are important centres of growth. Their ability to contribute effectively to the economy and meet the essential needs of the growing urban population is today constrained by the widening gap between the high quantum of resources required and the meagre resources at the disposal of the institutions engaged in the governance process.

Some of the salient problems are common to almost all urban areas. Chaotic conditions prevail on roads, railway stations and bus stands. Inadequate public transport systems, the poor quality of public transport vehicles and the proliferation of private vehicles have all made congestion and traffic jams a daily affair at peak hours. Intensifying the problems are the poor quality of roads, the road infrastructure and poor traffic management. The dire shortage of housing has led to the sky rocketing of land and rental costs and the mushrooming of unplanned/unauthorised constructions and slum settlements. Huge quantities of solid waste have piled up over the generations due to sheer neglect of waste management, and pollution and environmental degradation have become the theme of the day. Urban infrastructure and service levels have long been on the decline and there is, of course, the rising rate of crime that is concomitant to endemic poverty.

A number of reforms have been carried out from time to time to improve living conditions in urban areas (Figure 1.1). The empowerment and strengthening of urban local government institutions (ULGIs)/ municipalities was always an important component of the urban development reform agenda, since these entities are responsible for the governance of urban areas. The literature on evolution of urban local governments in India provides noteworthy information on the subject (Government of India, 1963).

Figure 1.1

Evolution of Urban Local Governments in India

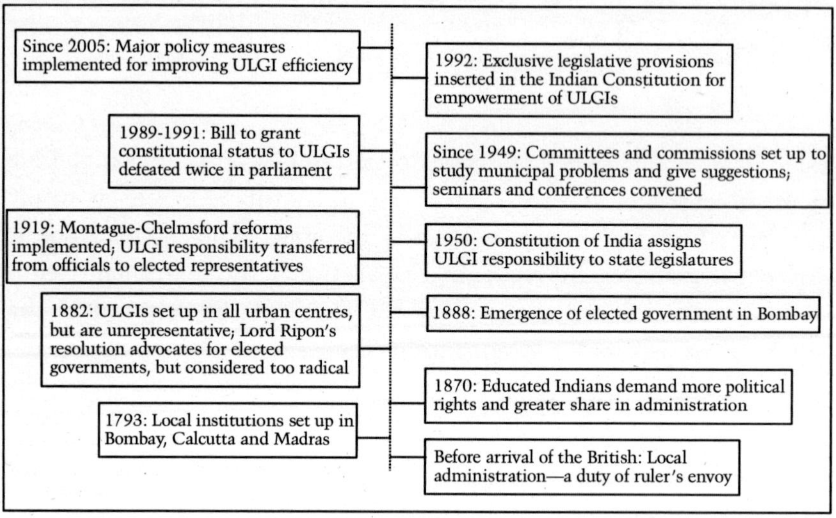

Before the advent of the British in India, administration of urban areas was the responsibility of representatives of the rulers. The British administration, however, felt the need to set up formal institutions of governance at the local level. By the Charter Act of 1793, local institutions were established in leading trading centres of Bombay, Calcutta and Madras, but they functioned merely as Courts of Record for civic and criminal cases. With the passage of time, the country experienced social and economic changes, and concepts such as social justice, equality and political rights assumed significance. Lord Mayo's resolution of 1870, aimed at decentralisation of administration and introduction of the principle of election in municipal laws, was not received well as the district officers did not favour the idea of extension of elective principle.

Local governments were set up in almost all urban centres by 1882 but they were not representative in nature. It was realised that issues such as the rising debt of the British Empire and aspirations and expectations of educated Indians could be met by involving the civil society in administration. Another attempt in this direction was made by Lord Ripon through his resolution of 1882, who pleaded for political education, functional devolution and constitution of elected committees in local governments. These ideas were, however, not acceptable to his successors who strongly favoured centralised control. At about the same time, the city of Bombay displayed emergence of an elected government with the enactment of Municipal Corporation Act, 1888.

A turning point in the efforts to constitute representative local governments came with the implementation of Montague-Chelmsford Reforms in 1919 that gave autonomy to provincial legislatures and also paved the way for reforms advocated by the Royal Commission on Decentralisation (1907-08). Though sufficient attention was not given towards strengthening municipal administration in the areas of drafting laws, method of recruitment, service conditions and training of personnel, augmenting local finances, etc., the important changes witnessed were transfer of local government responsibility from the district officer to a minister, widening of franchise for election to local bodies, and devolution of powers to revise rates of taxes.

India gained independence in 1947 and began to be governed by a Constitution, which provided for the distribution of powers between the Parliament and the state legislatures. In comparison to rural governments, municipal institutions did not find a place in the Constitution of India as the subject was exclusively assigned to the state governments. Thus, attempts to reform local governments were carried out through state legislative enactments.

Since 1948, several national-level committees and commissions have been appointed and conferences held to study municipal problems and give recommendations for their improvement. Important among these are the first conference of Ministers of Local Self-Government (1948), Local Finance Enquiry Committee (1949), Taxation Enquiry Commission (1953), Central Council of Local Self-Government (1954), annual conferences of the State Ministers of Town and Country Planning, All India Council of Mayors, and conferences of municipal corporations/commissioners, Committee of Ministers for Local Self-Government (1962), Committee on Rural-Urban Relationship (1963), Committee on Training of Municipal Employees (1963), Committee on Service Conditions of Municipal Employees (1965), Administrative Reforms Commission (1967),

Committee on Budgetary Reforms in Municipal Administration (1974), National Commission on Urbanisation (1985). The governments of various Indian states also undertook similar steps.

After nearly 45 years since independence, exclusive provisions for the empowerment of municipal institutions were inserted in the Indian Constitution. The initiative was widely criticised in the beginning since it was considered as an encroachment upon the rights of state governments. This is evident from the fact that a Municipality (*Nagarpalika*) Bill was defeated twice by a narrow margin in the Rajya Sabha (Council of States) between 1989 and 1991. The objective was finally achieved in 1992 with the enactment of the Constitution (74th Amendment) Act. The Act provides for significant reforms in the constitution, composition, powers and functioning of urban local governments. Thus, before the enactment of the Act, local government in urban areas was a state subject and its administration was entirely left in the control of the state legislature. Thereafter, municipalities continue to be governed by the respective state legislatures, but it has been made mandatory for the state governments to revise their municipal laws in accordance with the new Constitutional provisions.

Examples of important urban development initiatives undertaken by the Central government following the enactment of the Constitution (74th Amendment) Act in 1992 are the launch of the Jawaharlal Nehru National Urban Renewal Mission (JNNURM)[1] and the Urban Infrastructure Development Scheme for Small and Medium Towns (2005), launch of National Urban Information System Scheme (2006), formulation of a National Urban Transport Policy (2006), National Urban Housing and Habitat Policy (2007) and National Urban Sanitation Policy (2008) and an increased emphasis on regional planning and development. Due to these efforts, the development profile of many urban areas in the country is undergoing a noticeable change for the better.

---

1. Under the Mission, states and local governments can avail necessary financial, technical and institutional support for implementation of infrastructure projects and governance reforms. JNNURM comprises four components: (a) sub-mission on Urban Infrastructure and Governance (UIG); (b) sub-mission on Basic Services to Urban Poor (BSUP); (c) Urban Infrastructure Development Scheme for Small and Medium Towns (UIDSSMT) and (d) Integrated Housing and Slum Development Programme (IHSDP).

The Research Context

The form of urban local government in India has changed over time. As against the centralised nature of control and prevalence of rigid bureaucratic practices in the past, substantial efforts have been made to build municipal institutions based on democratic principles. The attempt is to improve local government efficiency by introducing and supporting innovative practices, and in guiding them towards success. In designing the urban development reform agenda, various elements of good urban governance (namely participation, rule of law, transparency, accountability, etc.) have been taken into consideration.

Unfortunately, most urban local governments in India are not demonstrating the desired level of efficiency in governance despite the implementation of recent reforms, as is made obvious from the poor quality of civic infrastructure and services available to the urban population. Visits to select municipal offices around the country have shown that these are not equipped properly to handle their duties efficiently and the working conditions of municipal functionaries are miserable at most places. In this situation, it becomes impossible for these agencies to gain higher revenues from their internal sources, or to provide an appreciably high level of services to the urban population, given their limited equipment and funds. As a result, the urban residents tend to shirk from paying their taxes because of the poor quality of civic services available to them.

An important conclusion which may be drawn from the current scenario is that many of the initiatives taken by the Centre are not penetrating down to the lowest level, and/or are being executed unprofessionally. Such a trend forebodes a further deterioration in the quality of urban life.

Some of the most complex issues in local-level governance observed today are imbalances in support by Centre and state governments to local governments, non-availability of data on vital development indicators required for the purpose of planning, acute shortage of funds for urban development, poor implementation of schemes, noteworthy intra-urban disparities, vested political interests, reluctance among the bureaucracy and elected representatives to adopt new practices, corruption, influence of social, economic and political factors on decision-making processes, ineffective women's participation in decision-making, violation of Municipal Act provisions, bias against maintenance of existing civic services, understaffing and low salary structures (Figure 1.2).

Figure 1.2

Constraints in the Governance Process

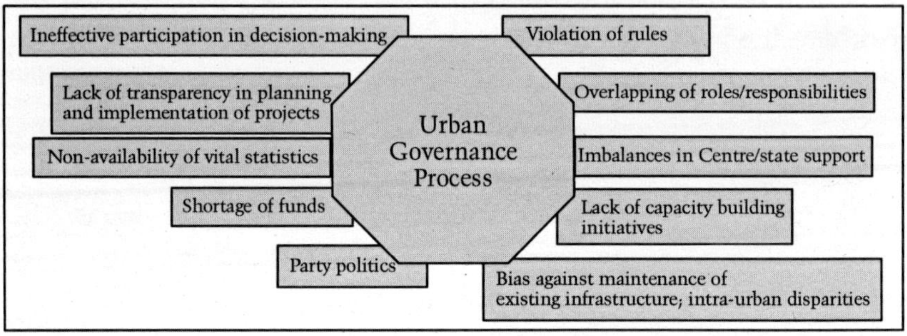

This research is centred around the hypothesis that the essence of democracy at local government level is yet to be achieved. The study shows that although a beginning has been made by way of constituting representative governments and by introducing innovative governance practices, citizen's participation in urban governance has been extremely limited. There seems to be little realisation that unless people are given sufficient opportunity to exercise equal control over matters which affect their interests, creation of equitable urban habitats would remain a challenge. For example, though elected members of municipalities possess voting powers to accept or reject a resolution, empirical research reveals that a minority of members are often oppressed by the majority. Similarly, lack of community participation in the formulation and implementation of urban development plans have resulted in striking urban disparities, as significant numbers of people do not have adequate access to basic necessities of life, such as shelter, infrastructure or civic services.

Objectives of the Study

In the context of recent government initiatives and the governance constraints, this study attempts to describe the: (a) main features of select reform measures implemented in municipalities; (b) important lessons learned from the adoption of new practices by the municipal functionaries in terms of success and/or failure and (c) policy measures needed to build stronger urban local government institutions. The purpose of conducting a study on this topic is to document the impact of novel practices which have been developed for improving governance at the local level, and to emphasise the fact that maximum benefits from any such initiative would be derived only when the local government institutions have been sufficiently strengthened.

Research Methodology

In the conduct of this research, the approach has been to appraise select Central government policy measures initiated to strengthen municipalities, and to examine the actions taken at the local level based on an analysis of suitable indicators and a selection of case studies. For instance, a survey of literature reveals that: at many places, major amendments have been made in the Municipal Acts; significant efforts are underway to enhance the knowledge of municipal functionaries; numerous civic services have been provided online on municipal websites and a number of financial reforms have been implemented for the municipalities across the country. Considering the significance of these initiatives, the study describes and evaluates various components of governance to understand precisely how municipalities, urban areas, and city residents are benefitting with the implementation of the recent policy measures. Based on personal interactions with the municipal functionaries and key respondents from training institutions, and data obtained from the selected case studies, prevailing problems in the governance process are highlighted and suitable policy suggestions have been put forward for improving local governance.

The four practices identified for review in the study are: (a) revision of municipal laws; (b) capacity building of municipal functionaries; (c) e-Governance initiatives in municipalities and (d) strengthening of municipal finance. These practices address the legislative, managerial, technological and financial dimensions of governance and each of them has been dealt with in a separate chapter. The selection of the above mentioned reform measures is based on a review of literature, published mainly by the

Ministry of Urban Development (MoUD), Finance Commission of India and the Planning Commission, indicating that these are significant policy reforms implemented in various states.

A further enquiry into each of the reforms is based on various other secondary sources of information, including the websites of Central ministries, the state governments' urban development and municipal administration departments, municipalities, training institutions and other national/international organisations (including the United Nations and the World Bank), Central and state governments publications, as also newsletters published by different organisations engaged in research on urban development and governance. Table 1.1 provides details on the components reviewed and analysed in this study, as well as the case studies selected for this research.

With respect to revision of municipal laws in Rajasthan, the State Municipalities Act, 2009 and the 2010 Ordinance have been reviewed to learn about the new amendments introduced following the launch of the Model Municipal Law by the MoUD. The selection of Rajasthan as a case study is based on the fact that it is one of the first states in the country that took steps to implement a new unified municipal law for all types of municipalities with distinct provisions for corporations. A study of the new legislative provisions reveals that the revised Act provides an opportunity for the introduction of important reforms such as public-private-people partnerships (PPPPs), housing and basic services for urban poor, commercialisation of projects, double entry system of accounting, pre-audit of expenditure, greater powers for resource mobilisation and enforcement of fines and penalties, and constitution of wards committees and zones.

The perceptions of trainers and trainees on the capacity building initiative in Nainital are understood by holding interviews with municipal functionaries (including the chairperson, executive officer, accountants, junior engineers and select councillors) and the faculty of the Uttarakhand Academy of Administration (UAoA). Nainital town has witnessed some positive changes in levels of basic infrastructure and the councils' revenue base, which makes it an important case to study. Moreover, the impact of a unique programme run by UAoA has not been documented till date. Thus,

Table 1.1

Scope of the Study

Reform Areas	*Components Reviewed and Analysed*	*Case Studies*
Revision of municipal laws	• Constitution (74th Amendment) Act, 1992 • Model Municipal Law	Rajasthan
Capacity building of municipal functionaries	• National government policy initiatives • Training institutions in states • Performance of municipality (based on case study) • Training arrangements • Perceptions of trainers and trainees	Nainital (Municipal Council and Uttarakhand Academy of Administration)
e-Governance initiatives in municipalities	• National government policy initiatives • Initiatives at the state level • Civic services available on the website (based on case study) • Impact of e-Governance initiative (based on indicators—property tax, birth/death certificates, tenders)	Delhi (Municipal Corporation)
Strengthening of municipal finance	• National government policy initiatives • Status of municipal finance (based on case study) • Financial reforms and their impact (based on indicators—accounting and audit, property tax, public-private partnerships)	Kolkata (Municipal Corporation)

the Nainital experience demonstrates simple and realistic ways of improving the quality of life.

In Delhi, officials from the information technology, property tax, engineering, factory and licensing departments of Municipal Corporation of Delhi, staff of the electronic service provider (i.e., Electronics Corporation of India Limited), and select municipal councillors were contacted to learn about the achievements and problems experienced in the expansion of online/internet-based civic services. The national capital of India assumes significance in this study because of its huge population size. By the year 2025, the urban agglomeration (UA) would rank second (after Tokyo) in the list of 30 largest UAs in the world ranked by population size (United Nations, 2009). Catering to the civic needs of nearly 30 million people will not be easy without use of appropriate technology. Thus, an in-depth assessment and documentation of e-Governance initiatives in Delhi offers an opportunity to other city governments to learn from and wisely implement such measures that have the ability to increase transparency and reduce corrupt practices.

Similarly in Kolkata, municipal functionaries (including the commissioner, and staff in the office of Comptroller of Municipal Finance and Accounts) were met for obtaining their feedback on the financial reforms and its impact on the financial condition of the corporation. The city corporation has experienced considerable growth in its revenue base, which makes it a case for studying the factors contributing to growth. This is also a useful way of demonstrating progress by a government following a unique Mayoral system with executive powers vested in the elected representatives.

Arrangement of the Study

The study is presented in six chapters. The introductory chapter explains the research design, including the study objectives, scope and methodology. The context of research is described by undertaking a brief survey of literature on the evolution of municipal institutions in India, current urban development problems, government initiatives and challenges of urban governance. Chapters Two, Three, Four, and Five describe in detail the four recent municipal reforms, and the achievements and problems experienced in implementing them. The concluding chapter presents a summary of the research findings, and lists down a set of suggestions for improving the performance of urban local government institutions in India. Information is also provided on several novel governance practices adopted in various parts of India and other developing countries for addressing complex urban problems.

References

Government of India (1966). *Report of the Rural-Urban Relationship Committee*, Vol. I & II. New Delhi: Ministry of Health and Family Planning.

———. (1963). "Augmentation of Financial Resources of Urban Local Bodies", Report of the Committee of Ministers constituted by the Central Council of Local Self-Government. New Delhi: Government of India.

———. (n.d.). *Five Year Plans* (various issues). New Delhi: Planning Commission.

Ministry of Urban Development (2010). *Annual report 2009-10*. New Delhi: Government of India.

United Nations (2009). *World Urbanisation Prospects: The 2009 Revision*. Department of Economic and Social Affairs, Population Division.

2 Revision of Municipal Laws

Urban local governments function according to the provisions of the act legislated for the purpose and local bye-laws. The act defines the criteria for the constitution of municipalities, their obligatory and discretionary duties, composition, procedure for reservation of seats and election to municipalities, the duties and powers of its functionaries, rules of conduct for meetings, sanctioning and execution of development works, preparation of budget estimates, appointment of committees, taxation rules and powers to impose penalties. In India, two types of municipal acts exist: (a) exclusively for a few large municipalities[1] (i.e., municipal corporations) and (b) a state municipal act which is applicable to other large, medium and small municipalities[2] functioning in a state (i.e., municipal corporations, municipal councils and *nagar panchayats*).[3] In addition, local governments formulate bye-laws for the furtherance of municipal administration. The municipal act is, therefore, a comprehensive guiding legal document for the local government officials, staff and the elected representatives, and bye-laws are framed to further clarify the administrative procedures.

Local governments have been established in various parts of India since 18th century onwards.[4] The acts by which these institutions are governed have been amended from time to time. Revision (or amendment) of municipal acts is a frequent practice which is undertaken due to various

1. For example, Delhi Municipal Corporation Act, 1957; Kolkata Municipal Corporation Act, 1980; Patna Municipal Corporation Act, 1951; etc.
2. Examples of State Municipal Acts are Assam Municipal Act, 1956; Haryana Municipal Act, 1973; Nagaland Municipal Act, 2001; Tripura Municipal Act, 1994; United Provinces Municipalities Act, 1916; Uttar Pradesh Municipal Corporations Act, 1959; West Bengal Municipal Act, 1993; etc.
3. Municipalities in union territories and cantonments are established by the Union laws.
4. These were first set up in Bombay, Calcutta and Madras by the Charter Act of 1793. Till 1858, as many as 20 towns were governed by a local government.

reasons, such as operational problems experienced by the municipal functionaries in respect of certain legislative provisions contained in the act, changes in government policies and changes in urban area characteristics. The purpose is to facilitate the effective functioning of local government departments.

In this chapter, two significant legislative reforms, namely the Constitution (74th Amendment) Act and the Model Municipal Law, initiated by the Indian government to strengthen governance are discussed in terms of their main features and the achievements at the local level. The concluding section offers some suggestions for overcoming the existing difficulties faced in the implementation and observance of municipal laws.

The Constitution (74th Amendment) Act, 1992

In ancient times of kings and *zamindars* (landholder/landowner), their representatives carried out the tasks of local administration. When India became a colony of the British Empire in the 19th century, district officers took over the affairs of the municipal bodies. The laws governing local bodies enacted during the period 1917 to 1937 failed to set up an effective system for day-to-day management of municipal affairs (GoI, 1966). After India's independence in 1947, the entire task of running local governments was handed over to the state authorities. The Constitution of India (1950) empowered state legislatures to decide on the structure, functions and powers to be entrusted to the local bodies, but in those early days, it gave inadequate reference to urban local governments. In the absence of constitutional recognition and clear statutory delineation of their powers, functions and resources, the municipal bodies remained neglected for several years. However, during this entire period, numerous efforts were made to strengthen their structure and functioning through legislative amendments and other reforms suggested by various commissions and committees, which yielded some positive results. It was also realised that local governance should not be the sole responsibility of the (higher levels of) government, and citizens' representatives should be given greater opportunity to participate in the functioning of these institutions because they had a first hand understanding of the local problems they faced in their day to day life.

The most significant achievement of the government in its efforts to reform municipal institutions in the country came with the enactment of the Constitution (74th Amendment) Act (CAA) in 1992.[5] The provisions of the Act have been listed in Part IX-A, which relates to municipalities, and have been inserted after Part IX of the Constitution, which relates to *panchayats* (i.e., rural local governments). The CAA, 1992 basically provides for the following amendments (Constitutional Provisions, 1999):

- Constitution of municipalities in every Indian state;
- Establishing a representative local government by reservation of seats for scheduled castes, scheduled tribes, backward class and women;
- Decentralisation of administration by the constitution of representative wards committees in urban areas, metropolitan planning committees (MPCs), and district planning committees (DPCs);
- Ensuring continuity in the term of municipalities by holding elections on time;
- Devolution of powers and responsibilities (including 18 functions listed in the 12th Schedule) upon municipalities to enable them to function as institutions of self-government and
- Strengthening the financial condition of municipalities by constitution of State Finance Commissions (SFCs), and audit of accounts.

The provisions of the CAA, 1992 were incorporated in the state/union Territory (UT) municipal acts. Subsequently, actions have been taken on implementation of the Act provisions in most states/UTs. In some states, such as West Bengal, some of the provisions already existed in the municipal laws of the state, and hence only the new provisions were incorporated (Annexure A-2.1).

These legislative reforms are noteworthy because they provide a constitutional basis for the creation of an efficient local government. Though local governments have been functioning for long, it is for the first

---

5. The act came into force with effect from June 1, 1993.

time that the state legislatures have been directed under the law to adopt, among other things, the principles of good urban governance. Thus, the marginalised groups are now participating in the decision-making process during municipal meetings and an election to constitute a municipality is held upon the completion of its term. The financial base of numerous municipalities has undergone a noticeable change with the constitution of SFCs and auditing of accounts. The progress in the implementation of other provisions, such as decentralisation of administration and devolution of powers and responsibilities, has however been slow in most states/UTs. Ranchi Municipal Corporation (Jharkhand) website (*www.ranchimunicipal.com*), for example, reports that there has been no real devolution of powers and functions. The Eleventh Five Year Plan of the Planning Commission (2007-2012), in this context, observes that, 'fiscal and administrative decentralisation have lagged behind political decentralisation'. To address these issues, the Central government has considered 'effective implementation of decentralisation initiatives as envisaged in CAA, 1992', as one of the state-level mandatory reforms within the Jawaharlal Nehru National Urban Renewal Mission's (JNNURM) agenda. Accordingly, the state governments and municipalities have been again directed to implement these reforms before applying for Central assistance for infrastructure projects under the Mission. The JNNURM database shows the progress achieved in the transfer of 18 functions listed under the 12th Schedule, and the constitution of DPCs and MPCs in various states. As on June 2, 2010, 11 states have reported transfer of functions to urban local bodies (ULBs) in accordance with the 12th Schedule of the Constitution. Twenty states have taken steps to establish DPCs and six states have constituted MPCs (*jnnurm.nic.in*, 2011).

The legislative reform measures carried out under the CAA, 1992 have been instrumental in highlighting a number of issues involved in local-level governance. An enquiry (MoUD, 2006) on the functioning of select medium and smaller-sized municipalities, state governments and SFCs, upon implementation of the Act provisions reveals that: (a) effective participation by the marginalised groups in the decision-making process during municipal meetings is generally not visible because of the influence of numerous social, economic and political factors, as well as the level of awareness among functionaries about the municipal acts' provisions (Aijaz,

2004); (b) there are frequent delays in the transfer of funds recommended by the SFCs; (c) several SFCs have failed to assess the resource requirements of local bodies (Finance Commission, 2004) and (d) expenditure norms for many services are not clearly defined.[6]

Model Municipal Law

Meanwhile, carrying forward the legislative reform process, the MoUD has initiated the task of refining the state municipal laws further for ensuring improved governance. A new law for municipalities, namely a Model Municipal Law (MML)[7] was formulated in 2003 to assist state legislatures in amending the municipal laws. Prior to the preparation of the new law, a study of several existing state municipal acts was carried out by the urban policymakers. This study revealed that the existing municipal laws impeded the urban reform process and accordingly it was suggested that there is an urgent need to amend the legislations. Some of the provisions reviewed by the policymakers to arrive at this decision include: financial, borrowing and taxation powers of municipalities; provisions for raising loans; penalties for violating rules and the functional domain of municipalities.

MML was prepared after holding extensive consultations with legal experts, practicing urban managers, and state government functionaries. The purpose is to: (i) achieve the goal of implementing the CAA, 1992 provisions in totality and (ii) pave the way for implementing new reforms through appropriate legislative amendments, without which it is envisaged that the problems confronting the municipalities may not be overcome. The MML document contains provisions relating to: (i) constitution and government; (ii) municipal revenue; (iii) urban environmental infrastructure and services; (iv) urban environmental management, community health and public safety; (v) regulatory jurisdiction and (vi)

6. This author has contributed extensively to two studies: (i) Impact of the Constitution (74th Amendment) Act, 1992 on the Urban Local Bodies: A Review and (ii) State Finance Commissions' Recommendations and Follow-up Actions Thereon, conducted for the MoUD, Government of India, during 2004-05.

7. The Model Municipal Law was put together by the MoUD with the support of The Times Research Foundation (Kolkata), which was the consultant, and the USAID, which provided technical and financial support.

powers, procedures, offences and penalties. Select provisions in respect of the above mentioned categories are listed in Annexure A-2.2. Some of the innovative legislative measures spelt out in the MML include: enhanced powers to elected councils through formation of Empowered Standing Committees; constitution of Cadres of Common Municipal Services; appointment of a State Municipal Vigilance Authority; constitution of a Municipal Establishment Audit Commission; classification of municipal functions under three categories—core municipal functions, functions assigned by government, and other functions; introduction of the latest system of accounting; provision for enhanced borrowing; private sector participation in financing, construction, maintenance and operation of infrastructure projects and civic services; authorising concessionaire to penalise users for non-payment of tariffs/user charges and preparation of an annual report on the environmental status of the municipal area (MoUD, 2010). Thus, MML serves as an exemplar for the state governments. They can choose from the new legislative measures to suit their needs and make the necessary amendments in the municipal laws for implementation.

The MoUD has undertaken several steps to facilitate follow-up action/implementation of the model law. First, a paper on the law was distributed to the state government functionaries. Subsequently, a national workshop was held in New Delhi on November 21, 2003 to generate awareness and give an impetus to the implementation process of various legislative provisions. This was followed by four regional workshops at Jaipur (September 17, 2004), Kolkata (November 19, 2004), Hyderabad (February 11, 2005) and Pune (April 8, 2005). A national roundtable was also organised in New Delhi on July 12, 2007 to review the status of its compliance in various states/UTs of India.

An assessment of different municipal acts shows that in most states of the country, multiple municipal acts are in use—one for the corporations and the second for all other municipalities (i.e., municipal councils and *nagar panchayats*). In seven states, a unified municipal law exists for municipal governance, and only four states have formulated a unified municipal law which is mainly based on MML (Table 2.1).

Table 2.1

Status of Municipal Acts

States with a Unified Municipal Law (Mainly Based on MML)	*States with a Unified Municipal Law*	*States with Multiple Municipal Laws*
Arunachal Pradesh, Bihar,[8] Rajasthan, Sikkim	Goa, Kerala, Manipur,[9] Meghalaya, Mizoram, Nagaland, Tripura	Andhra Pradesh, Assam, Chhattisgarh, Gujarat, Haryana, Himachal Pradesh, Jammu & Kashmir, Jharkhand, Karnataka, Madhya Pradesh, Maharashtra, Orissa, Punjab, Tamil Nadu, Uttarakhand, Uttar Pradesh, West Bengal

Source: Obtained from various state and local government websites in February 2011.

Case Study of Rajasthan Municipal Legislation

A comparison of the Rajasthan Municipalities Act, 1959 (as amended up to 2005), with the Rajasthan Municipalities Act, 2009 (a revised version of the 1959 Act) as well as the 2010 Ordinance reveals that numerous amendments have been made to the earlier act which now incorporates a number of provisions listed in the MML (GoR, 2005).[10] In particular, the revised act provides for the following:

- Two-tier structure of governance through municipality and ward committee, with distribution of functions, functionaries and funds for the two tiers;
- Direct election to the post of mayor and president/chairperson of municipalities;
- Well-defined municipal functions, devolution of all local government functions to municipalities, as also planning and various other

8. It is reported that after the passing of the Bihar Municipal Act, 2007, ULBs failed to meet the expectation of the people. See Yadav (2008).
9. Despite the Government of Manipur having already enacted the Manipur Municipalities Act, 1994, the State government was yet to devolve the powers and functions to the ULBs (The Sangai Express, December 20, 2008).
10. The Rajasthan Municipalities Act, 2009, Act No. 18 of 2009; The Rajasthan Municipalities (Amendment) Ordinance, 2010, No.1. An ordinance further to amend the Rajasthan Municipalities Act, 2009.

works to be undertaken by municipal bodies with minimum government interference;

- Integration of development plans and schemes of the municipal area with the district or regional development plan;
- Preparation of a municipal accounting manual by the state government containing details of financial matters and procedures in respect of municipalities; provision for conduct of special and internal audit of municipal accounts; formulation of a comprehensive debt limitation policy describing principles governing raising of loans by municipalities, limit of loans, rate of interest to be paid for such loans and terms and conditions, including the period of repayment;
- Planning, construction, operation, maintenance and management of commercial infrastructure projects through public or private sector agencies;
- Preparation of a city development plan by the municipality in consultation with all concerned officials/departments;
- Formation of a state municipalities union to examine issues of common interest and make suitable representations to the state government;
- Allotment of at least 20 per cent of plots or housing units in group housing or township projects to persons belonging to economically weaker section and low income group at concessional rates through cross-subsidisation of prices;
- Constitution of Basic Services to the Urban Poor Fund for the purpose of providing basic services to the urban poor including slum dwellers; earmarking of about 25 per cent of yearly budget grants of a municipality for the purpose.

Conclusion

Revision of municipal laws is a common practice. These have been amended from time to time by the legislatures ever since the acts have come into existence. The purpose of such interventions is to remove the flaws and strengthen the structure by empowering the functionaries for a smooth functioning of the institutions, as well as enhance the much needed funds, so that the municipalities are able to demonstrate an improved level of governance. In this chapter, two major legislative reforms implemented by the Indian government have been examined, namely the Constitution (74th Amendment) Act enacted in 1992, and a Model Municipal Law formulated and distributed to various state/UT government functionaries in October 2003.

The first initiative led to a noticeable change in local governance, since it had a constitutional basis. It was mandatory for the state/UT legislatures to insert the CAA, 1992 provisions in their respective acts/laws and to implement them. Significant progress was achieved, but the efforts to decentralise administration at the level of the ward and to devolve the powers, functions and funds from the state to municipal governments achieved limited success. This was mainly because the state government functionaries were reluctant to transfer their powers and because the municipal functionaries did not possess the expertise required to handle new and additional responsibilities.

The impact of the Model Municipal Law is yet to be felt, since it is a recent initiative and is not mandated by the Constitution. Hence, only a few state governments of India have revised their municipal acts based on MML provisions (Table 2.1). It is envisaged that the revised acts will facilitate state/UT governments in devolving more powers and funds to municipalities, clearly delineate the functional domain, and strengthen the revenue base by allowing them to: borrow funds, raise loans and tax-free bonds; impose fresh taxes, user charges, levies and surcharges, as also revise tax/service rates; introduce reforms in accounting practices; mortgage property to banks against which bank will give credit and encourage public-private-partnerships (PPPs). In short, the law attempts to address the grey areas which act as barriers in local-level governance.

In the context of the ongoing municipal legislative reform process, a major task for the national government is to ensure that the necessary support mechanism is put in place for the implementation as well as enforcement of new/existing laws. The situation at the moment is such that while there is considerable emphasis on the amendment/revision of municipal acts, implementation/enforcement of several laws is not taking place. The basic question, therefore, is: what are the difficulties involved in the implementation and enforcement of some municipal laws, and how can these be overcome? If there are vested interests both at the state and the local level, such as those pertaining to power-sharing arrangements, etc.,—as observed by many functionaries and scholars—these should be identified and suitably addressed. The other issue is related to the violation of existing laws, both by the functionaries and the citizens. There are numerous examples to demonstrate this fact. For instance, despite a fairly well-defined functional domain, in several parts of India's capital city the road surface continues to remain in a poor state for long periods, street lights and other road infrastructure are not provided, traffic is not regulated (many two-wheelers/cyclists can be seen moving on footpaths), public transport service is poor, solid waste is not removed, streets are not swept and there is a continuous growth of unplanned/unauthorised constructions and slum settlements. These problems continue to exist despite the existence of laws as well as multiple development agencies. In other towns and cities, the situation is worse. At some places, it is observed that there is strong opposition from the elected municipal representatives and the urban residents whenever certain legislative reform measures are introduced by the state/local authorities in respect of property tax assessment procedures, revision of tax rates and service charges, or promotion of public private partnerships in the delivery of civic services. Local political leaders and municipal staff often feel that they will loose their popularity and position if service rates are hiked, or private contractors are involved in municipal works.

With respect to strengthening the procedures involved in the implementation and enforcement of municipal legislations, this study recommends the following:

- Awareness programmes should be conducted for state/local government functionaries and the citizens on the significance of new legislative reforms and the implementation guidelines; ongoing municipal capacity building programmes should be accordingly designed.
- Independent municipal law monitoring agencies should be created at the national and state levels to assist and guide the law enforcement agencies at the local level.

- A detailed study should be undertaken on the practices adopted by existing law enforcing agencies, which should review the powers, responsibilities and problems of legal officials affiliated with municipalities, availability of staff and infrastructure required for enforcement purposes, etc., in order to identify and address the constraints.
- Fines/penalties should be compulsorily imposed on any citizen/functionary found violating a municipal law. Laws are violated due to several reasons, such as ignorance, vandalism, poor levels of infrastructure and services, political factors and corruption, among others. Take the case of solid waste removal. The sheer lethargy shown in its collection and the paucity of transportation and disposal facilities forces the citizens to get rid of their waste and garbage by dropping them at any place that suits them, such as open drains, road sides, vacant plots, etc. Similarly, due to the absence of footpaths, citizens are left with no option but to walk on the roads. These are just a few examples of the results of incomplete, inefficient and apathetic planning. The problem can be partly overcome by ensuring a planned and comprehensive development of urban areas, and by involving private agencies in the operation and maintenance of various basic urban infrastructure and services. Also, adherence to master plans/city development plans may be useful in overcoming many of the hurdles that come in the way of urban development.

Unless such measures are taken, the necessary municipal laws will never be implemented, or will continue to be violated both by the government functionaries, as well as the citizens. It may be concluded that the successful implementation of these legislative reforms remains a challenge. Only through planned and persistent efforts can this gigantic task be achieved.

References

Aijaz, R. (2004). "Urban Governance in Basic Civic Services – Case Study of Selected Centres in Meerut District of Uttar Pradesh". Unpublished PhD Thesis. New Delhi: Department of Regional Planning, School of Planning and Architecture.

Constitutional Provisions Relating to Village Panchayats and Municipalities in India (1999). Lucknow: Eastern Book Company.

Finance Commission (2004). *Report of the Twelfth Finance Commission (2005-2010)*. New Delhi: Government of India.

Government of India (1966). *Report of the Rural-Urban Relationship Committee*, Vol. I. New Delhi: Ministry of Health and Family Planning.

Ministry of Urban Development (2010). *Annual Report 2009-10*. New Delhi: Government of India.

———. (2006). *Report of the Working Group on Urban Development (Excluding Urban Transport), Urban Water Supply and Sanitation (Including Low Cost Sanitation, Sewerage and Solid Waste Management) and Urban Environment for Eleventh Five Year Plan (2007-2012)*. New Delhi: Government of India.

Ministry of Urban Development and Poverty Alleviation (2003a). *Model Municipal Law*. New Delhi: Government of India.

———. (2003b). *Policy Options for Framing Municipal Laws*. New Delhi: Government of India.

Government of Rajasthan (2005). *Municipal Law in Rajasthan* Volume 1 and 2, Revised Fourth Edition. Jaipur: Bafna Publishing House (The Rajasthan Municipalities Act, 1959).

Planning Commission. *Eleventh Five Year Plan 2007-2012*, Vol. III. New Delhi: Government of India.

———. *Draft Report of the Steering Committee on Urban Development for Eleventh Five Year Plan. (2007-2012)*. New Delhi: Government of India.

Yadav, S. (2008). "Act Soon to Bring Transparency in Bihar ULBs", published on August 19, 2008, iGovernment website.

Annexure A-2.1

Status Report on Conforming Legislations and Action Taken in West Bengal Following the Enactment of the Constitution (74th Amendment) Act, 1992

Mandate of the Constitution	*Action taken*
Article 243-Q envisages three types of municipalities: municipal corporations for large cities, municipal councils for smaller cities and towns, and *nagar panchayats* for areas in transition from 'rural' to 'urban'.	Much before the 74th CAA came into force, the ULBs of West Bengal were categorised into three types, i.e., corporations for large cities, municipalities for smaller cities and towns, and notified area authorities for transitional areas. Criteria for constitution of such three types of ULBs were provided in the state municipal laws. After the introduction of 74th CAA, the state government has classified its ULBs into three categories as envisaged in the Constitution. Presently there are six municipal corporations, 116 municipal councils (municipalities) and three notified areas (for transitional areas) in the state.
Article 243-R provides for filling up of all seats in the Municipal Councils mandatorily by direct election. Apart from this, there are provisions for representation in the Municipal Council of Members of Lok Sabha/ Legislative Assembly (with voting rights) representing wholly or partially constituencies in Municipal area and also of persons (without voting rights) having specialised knowledge or experience in municipal administration.	Since 1981, i.e., well before the 74th CAA was brought into force, general elections to the ULBs are being held at regular intervals and at present 122 ULBs of the state are run by the representatives directly elected by the people. General elections are going to be held in six ULBs, including three newly created municipalities, shortly, and thus all the 125 urban bodies of this state will have elected bodies by July 2002. Municipal laws have been amended to provide representation of persons having specialised knowledge or experience in municipal administration. No provisions have, however, been made for representation in the ULBs of the Members of the House of People and the Members of the Legislative Assembly of the state on the ground that representation of Members of the Lok Sabha or State Assembly with voting rights may lead to confusion.
Article 243-S prescribes constitution of Wards Committees for groups of wards mandatorily for cities with population more than 300,000.	State government has made provisions in municipal laws for constitution of Borough Committees consisting of not less than six contiguous wards mandatorily for municipal corporations and also for municipalities having population 300,000 or more and Ward Committee for each ward of each ULB irrespective of its population size. Manner of constitution and functions of Borough Committee and Ward Committees have been prescribed by rules.

contd...

...contd...

Mandate of the Constitution	*Action taken*
Article 243-T provides for reservation of seats (municipal constituencies) for scheduled castes (SC), scheduled tribes (ST) and women in municipal councils. The seats reserved for SCs & STs are to be in proportion to their population in the respective ULBs. Not less than 1/3rd of the seats are to be reserved for women. This Article also provides for reservations in the office of chairpersons for SC, ST, women and other backward classes of citizens.	The state government has made provisions for reservation of seats in ULBs in accordance with the Constitutional stipulation through the following enactments: 1. The West Bengal Municipal Elections Act, 1994. 2. The West Bengal Municipal Elections (Reservation of Seats) Rules, 1994. Legislature of the state has made provision in the Municipal Laws for reservation in the office of the chairperson.
Article 243-U stipulates that the term of office of the Municipal Council will be five years from the date appointed for its first meeting and no longer. Moreover, if a municipality is dissolved by the state government, election to the same must be held within a period of six months.	Required provisions have been made in the Municipal Laws of the State. General elections to the ULBs in this State are being held at regular interval since 1981, i.e., much before introduction of the 74th CAA. No ULB in this state was dissolved after the 74th CAA came into force and, therefore, holding elections to the dissolved ULB did not arise.
Article 243-V deals with the criteria for disqualification from being a municipal member and prescribes the minimum age of 21 years for contesting the elections.	Well before introduction of the 74th CAA, the State Legislature prescribed 21 years as minimum age for contesting municipal elections. Even the age of voters in the municipal elections was reduced from 21 to 18 in the year 1978, before the general elections to the ULBs in the year 1981. Necessary provisions have, however, been made in the municipal laws paying due regard to the Constitutional provisions.
Article 243-W: It is the mandate of the Constitution that the municipality as an institution of local self-government will prepare plans for economic development and social justice and perform such functions and implement such schemes as may be entrusted to them by the state government, including those in relation to the matters listed in the 12th Schedule of the Constitution.	Long before the 74th CAA came into force, almost all of the functions as specified in the 12th Schedule were incorporated in the municipal laws of this state. Very few necessary amendments were, however, incorporated in Municipal Acts as per amendments of the Constitution. Powers and functions of the municipalities have been categorised into two types, i.e.: (1) obligatory and (2) discretionary. Presently, the ULBs are performing almost all the functions except those relating to fire fighting.
Article 243-X deals with devolution of financial power to the ULBs by the state government through: (i) empowering the ULBs to impose tax, (ii) assigning to municipalities such taxes, duties tolls and fees levied and collected by the state government and (iii) grants-in-aid.	Well before introduction of the 74th CAA, the state government empowered the ULBs through enactment for imposition and collection of taxes and non-tax levied by the ULBs. The West Bengal Central Valuation Board was also set up with a view to attaining conformity and objectivity in valuations of lands and buildings in municipal areas. Apart from this, state government shares the

contd...

...contd...

Mandate of the Constitution	*Action taken*
	taxes levied and collected by it with the ULBs on the basis of the population size of the ULBs and other relevant criteria and also provides for grants-in-aid under various plan and non-plan heads. Since the existing municipal laws contain such provisions, the question of further amendment did not arise. State government has, however, taken necessary steps for devolution of funds to the ULBs on the basis of the recommendations of the Tenth/ Eleventh Finance Commission and the State Finance Commission.
Article 243-Y prescribed that the state governments are mandatorily required to constitute State Finance Commission in every five year which would recommend the devolution of taxes, charges, fees, tolls, duties, shared revenues and inter-governmental transfer to municipalities.	The State government constituted the first State Finance Commission by a Notification dated 30th May, 1994 and the said Commission submitted its recommendations in 1995, relating to devolution of state taxes, grants-in-aid and other matters, and the state government took action on the said recommendations. The second State Finance Commission was constituted on 14.7.2000 and it submitted its recommendations to the state government on 6.2.2002. The recommendations are now under examination of the Finance Department.
Article 243-Z prescribes maintenance of accounts by the municipalities and audit of such accounts.	Long before introduction of the 74th CAA, provisions had been there in the relevant municipal laws for maintenance of accounts and audit of the same by the Examiner of Local Accounts, which is a wing of the Accountant General of West Bengal. Apart from this, provisions were there in the prevailing laws for constitution of Accounts Committee and internal audit of municipal accounts to keep checks and balance on municipal accounts. Further amendment in the existing Municipal Laws, therefore, was not called for.
Article 243-ZA: Under this Article the State Governments are mandatorily required to constitute State Election Commissions to supervise, direct and control the process of preparing the electoral rolls and conducting the elections to the municipalities.	In accordance with the stipulation of the 74th CAA, the State Election Commission was constituted under the West Bengal State Election Commission Act, 1994 through a Notification. Preparation of electoral rolls and conduct of elections in respect of all the 125 ULBs of this state are undertaken under the superintendence, direction and control of the aforesaid Commission. The West Bengal Municipal Elections Act, 1994 was enacted for this purpose and the Rules [i.e., the West Bengal Municipal Elections (Registration of Electors) Rules, 1995 and the West Bengal Municipalities (Conduct of Election) Rules, 1995] were framed there under.
Article 243-ZB: This Article is applicable to Union Territories.	Not applicable to this state.

contd...

...contd...

Mandate of the Constitution	*Action taken*
Article 243-ZC: Provision for certain areas including Darjeeling Hill Council.	Necessary provisions have been made in the Municipal Act.
Article 243-ZD: This Article provides for constitution of District Planning Committee (DPC) for consolidating the plans prepared by the *panchayats* and municipalities in the district and for preparation of draft development plans for the district as a whole.	The West Bengal District Planning Committee Act, 1994 has been enacted by the state government wherein provisions have been made for the composition of the DPC, its term of office, powers, functions, etc. The state government has also prescribed rules for carrying out the purpose of the act. The District Planning Committees are in position and functioning in all the districts.
Article 243-ZE: Under this Article the state governments are mandatorily required to constitute a Metropolitan Planning Committee to prepare a draft development plan for the metropolitan area as a whole.	The state government has enacted the West Bengal Metropolitan Planning Committee Act in 1994 and framed Rules there under. The West Bengal Metropolitan Planning Committee has been constituted and is fully functional.

Source: Action Taken Report, obtained from the Department of Municipal Affairs, Government of West Bengal.

Annexure A-2.2

Select Legislative Reform Measures Proposed in the Model Municipal Law

Constitution and Government

New chapter on 'Constitution of Municipal Areas and Classification of Municipalities'; creation of a political executive; establishment of ward committee in each ward; appointment of 'statutory officers'; constitution of 'Cadres of Common Municipal Services'; setting up of a 'Municipal Service Commission for Municipal Corporation' and a 'State Municipal Service Commission for Municipal Councils and *Nagar Panchayats*'; appointment of a 'State Municipal Vigilance Authority'; constitution of a 'Municipal Establishment Audit Commission'; listing under the 'Functional Domain of Municipalities', 'Core municipal functions', 'Functions assigned by Government' and 'Other functions'.

Financial Management of Municipalities

Receipts and expenditures of municipalities may be kept under various heads of accounts including those for 'water supply, drainage and sewerage', 'solid waste management', 'road development and maintenance', 'slum services', 'commercial projects' and the 'general account'; under all the accounting heads, the 'revenue account' and the 'capital account' would be maintained separately; introduction of the latest system of accounting on the basis of a 'Municipal Accounting Manual'; preparation of a 'financial statement containing an income and expenditure account and receipts and payments account' as also of a 'balance sheet' of the assets and liabilities of any municipality; constitution of a 'Municipal Accounts Committee'; 'Credit Rating of Municipal Bonds' by credit rating agencies; a Report on 'Services Provided in a Subsidised Manner' proposed for indicating the 'extent of subsidy', the 'source from which the subsidy was met' and the 'beneficiaries' thereof, for water supply, disposal of sewage and solid wastes; a chapter on 'municipal property' provides for preparation and submission along with the budget estimates of an inventory of immovable municipal properties along with a statement on their optimum exploitation.

Municipal Revenue

A chapter on 'Sources of Internal Revenue' has been included to emphasise the need for enhancing the internal resource generation capacities of the municipalities from other sources too; 'area-linked system for determination of annual values', a progressive rate structure based on the 'straight line system', a surcharge on properties used for 'non-residential' purposes and an additional surcharge on 'rented properties' for the levy of property tax by the municipalities; separate rate structure specified for any land, hut or building in any slum; provisions for self-assessment of land and buildings by its owner or any person liable to pay the property tax or by the occupier; water tax and fire tax proposed; new tax proposed on 'deficits of parking spaces in non-residential buildings' by certain municipalities; advertisement tax would be levied depending upon the location, size and medium of advertisement including the advertisements in the transportation terminals; surcharge proposed for advertisements on display in any temporary congregation of whatever nature; surcharges proposed on taxes levied on entertainments under the relevant state laws and on consumption of electricity; toll proposed on heavy trucks and buses plying in any municipal area; a chapter on 'Commercial Projects' included in order to tap revenues.

Urban Environmental Infrastructure and Services

Municipality may, on its own or on the basis of a private sector participation agreement, promote the undertaking of any project involving a company, a firm, a society, a trust or any body corporate or any institutional, statutory or government agency in financing, construction, maintenance and operation of projects for supply of urban environmental infrastructure or services; municipalities may provide these services: water-supply, drainage and sewerage including trade effluents, solid wastes: including bio-medical wastes and hazardous wastes, communication systems including streets, street furniture, street lighting, traffic engineering schemes, parking lots and bus stops, and for provision of markets, commercial infrastructure and slaughter houses on their own, or arrange to have the same provided by other agencies under various types of private sector participation agreements; provisions have been made for levy of sewerage charges and sewerage cess, maintenance of complete survey maps, drawings and description of underground water mains, supply pipes, drains, sewers, etc.; prohibitions have been made regarding construction of building, wall, fence or other structure or any railway, or private street on any municipal drain or any water main, as also for sanction of building plans unless such plans conform to the requirements under the rules and regulations for water supply, drainage and sewerage, and availability of privy and urinal accommodation within the premises; new chapter has been introduced on the constitution of and functions of a State Municipal Regulatory Commission.

Urban Environmental Management, Community Health and Public Safety

A chapter is included on 'Local Agenda for Urban Environmental Management' and separate chapters have been devoted to 'Environmental Sanitation and Community Health', 'Restraint of Infection', 'Disposal of the Dead' and 'Urban Forestry, Parks, Gardens, Trees and Playgrounds'; provisions have been made for 'preparation and submission of an Annual Report on the Environmental Status' of the municipal area at the time of submission of the budget estimates.

Regulatory Jurisdiction

Chapters are included on 'Development Plans', 'Improvement', 'Public Streets', 'Buildings', 'Municipal Licences', 'Vital Statistics', 'Disaster Management' and 'Industrial Townships'; a clause has been included to provide for representation of the municipality in the District Planning Committee(s) or the Metropolitan Planning Committee(s).

Source: MoUD (2003b).

3 Capacity Building of Municipal Functionaries

Developing countries the world over are trying to improve the quality of life in urban areas by strengthening the local government institutions. A significant initiative undertaken to achieve this challenging goal is the task of capacity building of the local government (or municipal) functionaries. It is widely agreed that many of the problems of governance experienced by the municipal functionaries can be overcome by broadening their knowledge base. The rationale for this emphasis on capacity building is that while urban management is becoming increasingly complex, the required effort is not being made to widen the understanding of actors involved in the process of governance (Amos, 1989). Thus, when new reform measures such as decentralisation or private sector participation are initiated, these often meet with limited success because the functionaries are not prepared for handling new and additional responsibilities.

Many governments view capacity building as an important strategy component. This is evident from a review of literature. For instance, the UN Habitat's Training and Capacity Building Branch (TCBB) collaborates with national and city governments, local authorities, and civil society organisations in various parts of the world to build core skills in diverse areas, such as leadership, financial management, local economic development, participatory planning, budgeting, gender mainstreaming, conflict management, etc. It also develops training manuals and tools for evaluating the impact of training on a participant's job performance and how that impact translates effectively into the betterment of a human settlement (Tuts, 2006).

A review of capacity building initiatives undertaken in some developing countries, including Angola, Burkina Faso, Cambodia, Egypt,

---

This chapter is an elaborate version of a research article written by the author. The article was published in the *Habitat International Journal* 34(4): 386-91, October 2010, published by Elsevier.

Ethiopia, Mongolia, etc., reveals that due to the financial and technical support offered by the UN Habitat, improvements are observed in basic urban sectors, such as city management, housing, slum upgrading, infrastructure and services, educational facilities, waste management, employment generation and youth empowerment. In some cities, namely Addis Ababa (Ethiopia), Luxor (Egypt), Phnom Penh (Cambodia), representatives from the Central and local governments, private sector, civil society, community organisations and donor community were encouraged to participate in the urban governance process (UN Habitat, 2009). In Udon Thani (Thailand), the communities have partnered with municipal officials in identifying all slums and squatter settlements, and drawn up action plans for their improvement (Hogan, 2006). Furthermore, other major urban development lending agencies including the World Bank and the Asian Development Bank (ADB) invest in projects aimed at strengthening the capacity of municipal governments so that they are in a position to provide better infrastructure, services and employment opportunities to the growing urban population (ADB, 2009). For example, municipal strengthening is an important component of the World Bank funded Rio Grande Do Sul Integrated Municipal Development Programme Project (Brazil), under which activities related to improving municipal capacity are being funded to plan, appraise, finance, implement, monitor and evaluate the infrastructure and the local economic development investments in select municipalities of Brazil (World Bank, 2009). An appraisal report of a capacity building project implemented in Indonesia noted: '(a) improved capacity of provincial and local governments for urban management; (b) notable improvements in urban infrastructure and services investments; involvement of public, private and community partnerships; resource revenues; maintenance budgets for roads, drains and other urban infrastructure; and cost recovery for solid waste; (c) the newly established financial management system being utilised by participating local governments and water service companies; (d) enhanced private sector and community participation in planning, policy making, and budgeting through the Projects' Urban Development Coordination Forums and; (e) increased participation of non-government institutions' (ADB, 2009).

There are also concerns over the weak capabilities of institutes engaged in training and capacity building activities. To address such issues, a network of local government training and research institutes (LOGOTRI) in Asia and the Pacific has been developed by the UNESCAP with the objective of encouraging advisory services, exchange of staff and information, joint training workshops, comparative research and documentation of practices (UNESCAP, 2009). Similarly, city/municipal partnerships (or city to city cooperation) across nations is increasingly being explored as an approach for promoting the exchange of ideas and knowledge and thus improve local government performance (Bontenbal, 2009).

The Indian government is concerned over the poor functioning of urban local government institutions. An appraisal of the management and finance practices of select municipalities provides evidence on the nature of constraints in local governance processes. Some of the most common problems include influence of numerous social, economic and political factors on the municipal decision-making process, ineffective participation of elected women councillors in municipal affairs, ignorance among functionaries on various municipal matters, delays in convening municipal meetings, minutes of meetings going unrecorded, factionalism among councillors during decision-making, lack of transparency in sharing information on project planning and implementation, corruption, low cost recovery from taxes and non-taxes, and a high dependence on external sources of finance. Such problems adversely affect the quality of life in many urban areas of India (Aijaz, 2007).

At various places in the country, efforts are being made to strengthen municipal work practices by conducting orientation programmes for municipal functionaries (i.e., officials and elected representatives). The objective is to raise their awareness levels by educating them on various innovative urban governance practices which have been successfully used in India and other developing countries, so that they are able to deal effectively with the growing problems in the governance of urban areas. Adequate information is, however, not available on the practices followed by the training institutions in building the capacity of municipal functionaries in India. Moreover, significant efforts have not been made to illustrate the usefulness of such initiatives and the underlying problems. The purpose of this chapter is to provide information on such partially explored areas, which would be of immense use to the urban policymakers and will facilitate them in outlining future policy directions.

This chapter is divided into five sections. The first section provides a brief introduction on capacity building measures initiated in various parts of the world to improve the performance of urban local government institutions. The purpose and scope of this chapter is also described. The second section contains information on significant initiatives undertaken by the Indian government to promote capacity building programmes at the municipal level. Sections three and four present a case study of a training institution, and the impact of capacity building efforts. This includes a review of: training arrangements for municipal functionaries; thrust areas of training; methodology used in the conduct of programmes; participants, trainers and sponsors; exposure given to the faculty engaged in training; funding pattern for training programmes; perceptions of trainers and trainees on the quality of training and the impact of capacity building efforts. Empirical evidence is provided from Nainital, a hill town[1] situated in the North Indian state of Uttarakhand, where the Uttarakhand Academy of Administration (UAoA) is playing an important role in raising the awareness of municipal functionaries in the state. The concluding section discusses the important lessons learned and throws light on the actions required to make the capacity building initiative successful.

Municipal Capacity Building Initiatives in India

The Government of India appointed a Committee on the Training of Municipal Employees in 1963. It was felt that local-level functionaries should be exposed to various options open to them for overcoming local problems. This committee recommended the setting up of training institutes at the national and state levels. Subsequently, a number of institutes were established by the Indian government at different points of time to train state government officers working in different departments. Gradually, the institutes began to offer courses on local government topics

---

1. Census data for the year 2001 show that Nainital recorded a total population of 38,630 and a geographical area of 11.73 sq kms. (Census of India, 2001, Final Population Totals and Primary Census Abstract). The town is governed by a Municipal Council as per the provisions of the United Provinces Municipalities Act, 1916. The Council also relies on the *Bye-laws, Rules, Regulations of the Nainital Municipality* published by the order of the Municipal Board, Nainital in August 1966 and amended from time to time. Nainital municipality was first constituted on October 3, 1850, and was again reconstituted under Act XV of 1873. The present Council has formed 13 municipal wards in the town for administrative purposes.

Table 3.1

Prominent Institutions Imparting Training to Municipal Functionaries in India

Name of State/ Union Territory	*Name of Training Institution*
States	
Andhra Pradesh	AIILSG, Visakhapatnam; Administrative Staff College of India, Hyderabad; Centre for Good Governance, Hyderabad; CMA, Hyderabad; Dr. Marri Channa Reddy Human Resource Development Institute of Andhra Pradesh, Hyderabad; RCUES, Hyderabad
Assam	Assam Administrative Staff College, Guwahati
Goa	AIILSG, Panaji
Gujarat	AIILSG, Ahmedabad, Rajkot, Surat, Vadodara; CMA, Ahmedabad
Haryana	Haryana Institute of Public Administration, Gurgaon
Himachal Pradesh	Himachal Pradesh Institute of Public Administration, Shimla
Jammu & Kashmir	Jammu & Kashmir Institute of Management, Public Administration and Rural Development (Main Campus in Srinagar and Regional Centre in Jammu)
Karnataka	AIILSG, Bengaluru, Belgaum; CMA, Bengaluru; State Institute for Urban Development, Mysore
Kerala	Kerala Institute of Local Administration, Thrissur; AIILSG, Cochin, Thiruvananthapuram
Madhya Pradesh	AIILSG, Bhopal, Indore; CMA, Bhopal; Noronha Academy of Administration and Management, Bhopal
Maharashtra	AIILSG centres at Akola, Jalgaon, Kalyan, Kolhapur, Mumbai, Nagpur, Nashik, Navi Mumbai, Pune, Shrirampur, Solapur; CMA, Mumbai; Yashwantrao Chavan Academy of Development Administration, Pune
Orissa	CMA, Bhubaneswar; AIILSG, Bhubaneswar
Rajasthan	AIILSG, Jaipur, Jodhpur; CMA, Jaipur; Harish Chandra Mathur Rajasthan State Institute of Public Administration, Jaipur
Tamil Nadu	CMA, Chennai
Uttarakhand	CMA, Dehradun; Uttarakhand Academy of Administration, Nainital
Uttar Pradesh	AIILSG, Lucknow; RCUES, Lucknow
West Bengal	Administrative Training Institute, Kolkata; CMA, Kolkata; Institute of Local Government and Urban Studies, Kolkata; Mega Cities Association, Kolkata
Union Territories	
Chandigarh	Centre for Research in Rural and Industrial Development, Chandigarh; CMA Punjab
Delhi	AIILSG; Association of Municipalities and Development Authorities; Human Settlement Management Institute; Indian Institute of Public Administration
Puducherry	AIILSG

Note: AIILSG – All India Institute of Local Self-Government; CMA – City Managers' Association; RCUES – Regional Centre for Urban and Environmental Studies.

Source: Various training institution websites.

for municipal functionaries. On the other hand, some institutes were set up exclusively to meet the capacity building requirements of local government functionaries. The names of prominent institutions and their location are provided in Table 3.1. One institution that focusses only on matters relating to municipal administration is the All India Institute of Local Self-Government (AIILSG). This institute, established in 1926, operates in various parts of the country through a network of regional centres and sub-centres. The centres undertake research, organise and conduct specialised diploma courses, seminars, conferences, and provide an open forum for officials and non-official members of municipalities. Similarly, a network of City Managers' Association (CMA) was created in 1997 with the financial support of USAID/USAEP, and with technical support of the International City/County Management Association based in Washington DC, USA. CMAs are membership-based associations of city managers, urban sector professionals, academic institutes and non-government organisations, established in various Indian cities with the objective of strengthening and enhancing the capacities of municipalities and other city level agencies.

In addition to setting up these institutions in different parts of the country and creating municipal networks, some other important measures have been taken. For instance, the MoUD (2006a) initiated a number of activities[2] aimed at promoting municipal capacity building in India. The Ministry also supports three Regional Centres for Urban and Environmental Studies (RCUES) situated at Hyderabad, Lucknow and Mumbai, and the Centre for Urban Studies at Indian Institute of Public Administration in New Delhi. These centres undertake research and training activities in the areas of urban development, local self-government, urban management, water supply and sanitation, property tax, municipal audit and accounting, public housing and low cost sanitation, and urban poverty alleviation programmes. For this purpose, a sum of Rs 35.10 million was sanctioned by the Ministry during the financial year 2006-07, which was increased to 50 million in 2009-10. It is reported that as many

2. Three significant municipal capacity building events held at the national level include: Training of Trainers (ToT) Workshop on Leadership and Management during June 29-30, 2005 at New Delhi; National Seminar on Strengthening Training and Capacity Building in the Urban Sector during September 2-3, 2005 at Pune; Training Workshop for Municipal Functionaries on JNNURM during May 9-12, 2006 at New Delhi.

as 83 training courses/seminars/workshops have been conducted during the period 2009-10 (MoUD, 2009; 2010). Second, a project on 'capacity building for decentralised urban governance' was launched in November 2006 by the Ministry in collaboration with UNDP (MoUD, 2006b). Under this project,[3] 16 city governments, four each in the states of Kerala, Orissa, Rajasthan and Uttar Pradesh, have been extended support through state-level implementing agencies[4] and in close consultation with respective state governments, in the areas of property tax, accounting procedures, and preparation of city development plans (UNDP, 2007). Third, the Ministry has initiated a programme for training women councillors. For this purpose, state governments are required to nominate one state-level institute for conducting training programmes of three days duration. Financial aid at the rate of Rs 1,000 per day per participant is provided to the institutions. In addition, the institutes are also given grants of up to Rs 500,000 for preparation of training modules. The total expenditure involved in the conduct of training programmes is shared between the Central and state government on 50:50 basis (MoUD, 2006a). Another significant initiative under a major urban renewal programme[5] is the allocation of funds for conducting rapid training workshops in cities which are lagging behind in urban development. Recent statistics show that about 2,000 elected representatives and 1,800 municipal and parastatal staff have participated in the workshops (MoUD, 2009; 2010). The Ministry also supports a Programme Management Unit at the state level to strengthen the capacity of state level nodal agencies (SLNAs) for effective implementation of projects and reforms under JNNURM. More recently, a Peer Experience and Reflective Learning (PEARL) programme has been launched with the support of the Ministry to foster cross-learning among cities and institutions.

---

3. An amount of US $2 million (approx. Rs 90 million) was earmarked and the project was expected to be completed by end of March 2008. See MoUD (2006b: 22).
4. The four state-level implementing agencies are: (i) Regional Centre for Urban and Environmental Studies, Lucknow (Uttar Pradesh); (ii) Xavier's Institute of Management, Bhubaneswar (Orissa); (iii) Kerala Institute of Local Administration (KILA), Thrissur (Kerala) and (iv) Rajasthan Urban Infrastructure Finance and Development Corporation (Rajasthan).
5. Namely the Jawaharlal Nehru National Urban Renewal Mission (JNNURM).

Case Study of a Training Institution in Nainital

The Uttarakhand Academy of Administration (UAoA) is a state-level training institute situated in Nainital. It was established[6] with the main objective of imparting professional training to state government officers[7] working in various departments, to enhance their skills and prepare them for challenging and complex tasks. The Academy also conducts urban research and organises training programmes for municipal functionaries in the state. The training and capacity building activities are coordinated by the Academy's Centre for Good Governance (CGG), and for this purpose the Centre collaborates with various national and international agencies/organisations, such as the Ministry of Urban Development, Ministry of Rural Development, Ministry of Agriculture, Department of Personnel and Training, Government of Uttarakhand, Housing and Urban Development Corporation, National Institute of Urban Affairs, Human Settlement Management Institute, the World Bank, USAID and the British Council. During the last three years (2005-06 to 2007-08), more than 200 training programmes have been organised by CGG in which over 5,500 municipal functionaries from different municipalities in the state have participated. Several programmes have been conducted with the support of government of India, the state government of Uttarakhand and international organisations especially for women chairpersons and councillors to enable them to participate effectively in the decision-making and implementation processes (Table 3.2). The following thrust areas of training are identified keeping in view the local issues and the target group:

- Leadership and decision-making.
- Solid waste management and environment.

---

6. The institute was formerly established as an Officer's Training School (OTS) at Allahabad, Uttar Pradesh in 1951. The OTS was shifted to Nainital in 1971, and its role was enlarged. Owing to its enlarged agenda, it was renamed as Administrative Training Institute in 1974. The institute was subsequently elevated to the status of UP Academy of Administration in 1988. After the reorganisation of Uttar Pradesh state in November 2000, the Government of Uttarakhand renamed it as Uttarakhand Academy of Administration in 2001.
7. Such as Indian Administrative Service officers, Provincial Civil Service (Executive) officers, Provincial Judicial Service officers, Group A and B officers from various government departments, etc.

- Public-private partnership (PPP) in infrastructure management.
- Basic services for urban poor.
- Community mobilisation and resource management.
- Financial management and resource mobilisation.
- Preparation of detailed infrastructure project reports.

The Academy has developed a course curriculum for conducting the programmes. Moreover, training modules and manuals formulated by UN Habitat on numerous topics, including financing urban infrastructure, resource mobilisation, project development, municipal budgeting and accounting, etc., are also used. During a training workshop, problems faced by the municipal functionaries in their day to day work are discussed with the faculty and solutions are identified. A variety of methods are used to make the workshop effective. At the beginning of each workshop, a programme guide is distributed to the participants. This booklet provides useful information on the theme of the workshop, its schedule and purpose, target group, internal and external faculty involved in delivering lectures, and a profile of the Academy, including the facilities available. This is followed by interactive lecture sessions conducted by internal/ external faculty on various topics related to the broad theme of the workshop. Field visits and documentaries are other equally significant components of a workshop. During lectures and in the programme guide, there is a reference to case studies on India and other developing countries, showing innovative methods that have been used to improve the functioning of municipalities. On conclusion of the workshop, an assessment exercise is conducted to understand the perceptions of participants on the quality of training programmes.

There are a total of 21 faculty members in the Academy possessing expertise in diverse fields, such as public administration, economics, finance, gender, governance, information technology and disaster management (Table 3.3). The director of the Academy is also the chief executive officer (CEO) of the Centre for Good Governance. The Academy also encourages its internal training faculty to participate in various national/state-level workshops organised at different places in India, where examples of good urban governance are discussed and shared by

Table 3.2

Training Programmes Conducted by the Centre for Good Governance, Nainital

Description of Item	*Training Programme Details*
	1. *Workshop on Leadership and Decision-Making*
Duration	14-16 February 2005 (three days)
Target group	Elected councillors of various municipal councils and *nagar panchayats* in the state of Uttarakhand
Trainers	Internal: Academy director; coordinator and project manager, Urban Affairs; External: Assistant Appraisal officer, HUDCO, Dehradun
Sponsor	Human Settlement Management Institute (HSMI), New Delhi
	2. *Solid Waste Management and Environment*
Duration; No. of participants	26-30 April 2005 (five days); 12 participants
Target group	Some representatives of Kumaon and Garhwal divisions; Elected chairpersons and councillors of municipal councils and *nagar panchayats* in the state of Uttarakhand; municipal officials engaged in solid waste management
Trainers	Internal: Academy director; coordinator and project manager, Urban Affairs; External: Chief medical officer, Nainital; faculty, Kumaon University, Nainital; executive officer, Municipal Council, Haldwani
Sponsor	Department of Personnel and Training, Government of India; NIUA, New Delhi
	3. *Public-Private-Partnership in Infrastructure Management*
Duration; No. of participants	24-28 May 2005 (five days); 13 participants
Target group	Elected representatives of municipalities in the state; senior officers of municipal councils and *nagar panchayats* engaged in infrastructure operation and maintenance
Trainers	Internal: Academy director; academy joint director; project director and senior project manager, Urban Affairs; External: Chairperson, Municipal Council, Rishikesh; executive officer, Municipal Council, Haldwani
Sponsor	NIUA, New Delhi
	4. *Refresher Course on Basic Services for Urban Poor*
Duration; No. of participants	22-24 August 2005 (three days); 22 participants
Target group	Chairpersons of various municipalities in the state of Uttarakhand
Trainers	Internal: Academy director; Academy additional director; project director and senior project manager, Urban Affairs; External: Chairperson, State Finance Commission, Uttarakhand Government; representative, Public Service Commission, Uttarakhand Government; director, Ministry of Urban Development, Government of India; director, Urban Development, Uttarakhand Government
Sponsor	NIUA, New Delhi

contd...

...contd...

Description of Item	*Training Programme Details*
	5. *Community Mobilisation and Resource Management in Operation and Maintenance*
Duration; No. of participants	29 August–2 September 2005 (five days); 11 participants
Target group	Elected councillors (male and female) of various municipalities in the state of Uttarakhand
Trainers	Internal: Academy director; Academy additional director; academy joint director; project director and senior project manager, urban affairs; academy officer on special duty; External: Director, Urban Development, Uttarakhand Government
Sponsor	Department of Personnel and Training, Government of India; NIUA, New Delhi
	6. *Financial Management and Resource Mobilisation*
Duration	3-7 October 2005 (five days)
Target group	Municipal Officials (i.e., Accountant, Engineer) of various municipalities in the state of Uttarakhand
Trainers	Internal: Academy director; Academy additional director; academy joint director; project director and senior project manager, Urban Affairs; External: Faculty, HSMI, New Delhi; representative, HUDCO Regional Office, Dehradun
Sponsor	Department of Personnel and Training, Government of India

Source: Programme guide distributed to the target group, Centre for Good Governance, UAoA, Nainital.

Table 3.3

Faculty Profile, Uttarakhand Academy of Administration, Nainital

S. No.	*Designation of Faculty*	*Number of Faculty*	*Area of Specialisation*
1	Director	1	Public administration
2	Additional director	1	Public administration
3	Joint director	5	Public administration, finance, marketing
4	Deputy director	4	Information technology, economics, revenue, finance
5	Assistant director	3	Information technology, finance
6	Officer on special duty	2	Public administration, gender
7	Social development specialist	1	Participatory governance
8	Monitoring and evaluation specialist	1	Rural and urban development, Natural resource management
9	Capacity building specialist	1	Governance
10	Communication and water/ sanitation engineer	1	Communication, water and sanitation
11	Associate professor	1	Disaster management, governance

Source: Website of Uttarakhand Academy of Administration (*www.uaoa.in*), February 2011.

distinguished urban professionals. An equally important event is the training network institutions' review meeting organised from time to time to share the experience of representatives from various training institutions in the country. The purpose of holding such events is to increase the awareness of trainers on the solutions available to overcome complex issues of governance. In addition to the internal faculty, experts/resource persons affiliated with prominent academic institutions in India are frequently invited to deliver lectures on a wide variety of themes.

Table 3.4

Training and Recreational Facilities, Uttarakhand Academy of Administration, Nainital

S. No.	*Facility*	*Details*
1	Training rooms	10 class rooms, 2 conference halls, 1 seminar room, one auditorium (capacity of 200 persons), with latest training equipment, such as projectors, computers, public address system, collar mike, white boards, pin up boards, flip chart boards, etc.
2	Conference facility	Academy provides conference facilities on payment basis for organising capacity building activities. This includes a complete package of hall/rooms for the event, audio-visual, data projection equipment, computers, boarding, lodging, recreation and transport facilities.
3	HUDCO building centre	For demonstration of low cost and earthquake resistant house construction technology to the trainees.
4	Library	Collection of 86,225 books, international and national journals, periodicals, recent studies and documents of World Bank, UNICEF, UNDP, etc.
5	Computer lab	A well-equipped computer lab and internet facility. Computers with 24 hours internet facility are also available in all hostel rooms.
6	Lodging	The Academy has two hostels, namely Gangotri and Yamunotri and one guest house, namely Alaknanda, which can accommodate about 150 participants/guests at a time on a sharing basis.
7	Mess	The Academy has a well-maintained mess, which offers quality food service.
8	Sports and recreation	The Academy provides a number of facilities for sports and recreation—billiards, badminton, table and lawn tennis, gymnasium, chess, etc.
9	Open space/lawn	For open air activities—high tea, campfire, etc.

Source: Uttarakhand Academy of Administration (*www.uaoa.in*), February 2011; Personal observation.

The Academy is also equipped with suitable infrastructure for conducting training programmes. This includes class rooms, conference room, auditorium, library, computer lab and lodging facility. Sports and other recreational facilities are also available to participants (Table 3.4).

Most municipalities in the state of Uttarakhand do not have sufficient funds to bear the cost of participating in training programmes. Due to this reason, the Academy has tied up with some funding agencies. The general practice is that the Academy signs an agreement with the agency, and the costs are shared as per the terms and conditions of the contract. For example, the USAID has collaborated with the Ministry of Urban Development and provides financial and technical support to the Academy. This is a significant initiative under the Indo-USAID Financial Institutions Reform and Expansion (FIRE-Debt) Programme, aimed at strengthening municipalities in a number of Indian states. USAID has tied up with the National Institute of Urban Affairs (NIUA), which is the nominee and designated technical representative of the Ministry of Urban Development, to facilitate in the organisation and coordination of municipal capacity building programmes (Figure 3.1). Thus, a Memorandum of Understanding has been signed between NIUA and the Academy, according to which NIUA, on behalf of USAID, provides a partial financial support of up to 67 per cent of the total cost of each training workshop with a specified maximum limit (of about Rs 100,000). It is a mandatory requirement for the Academy to submit the following to the NIUA: (i) biannual monthly training calendars at the beginning of every financial year for approval and (ii) proposal and budget estimate for each training workshop at least one month before the commencement of the workshop, specifying the estimate in terms of line items of expenditure, number of participants, duration of the workshop, and the course structure. The Academy is then eligible for an advance of up to 50 per cent of the total cost. The balance amount is reimbursed by the NIUA upon the conclusion of the workshop and within a period of three months, after receiving a duly certified utilisation certificate along with the: (i) total expenditure statement for each workshop; (ii) list of participants, including their names, complete addresses and telephone numbers; (iii) workshop summary report and (iv) the schedule of the training workshop.

Figure 3.1

Arrangement of Funds for Conducting Training Workshops, Uttarakhand Academy of Administration, Nainital

Collaboration between Ministry of Urban Development (MoUD) and USAID

- MoUD is represented by National Institute of Urban Affairs (NIUA)

↓

Memorandum of Understanding

- Signed between training institution and NIUA
- 67% of total cost of training workshop provided by NIUA (on behalf of USAID)
- Limit: INR 100,000

↓

Eligibility conditions for release of 50% advance amount

- Biannual monthly training calendars at beginning of each financial year
- Proposal and budget for each workshop one month before the commencement of the workshop
- Proposal to include items of expenditure, estimated number of participants, workshop duration, course structure

↓

Eligibility conditions for release of balance amount

- Duly certified utilisation certificate
- Total expenditure statement
- List of participants (including names, addresses and phone numbers)
- Workshop summary report
- Training workshop timetable/schedule

Impact of Capacity Building Programmes

The trainers and the trainees were interviewed by this author in order to understand their views on the capacity building programmes organised by the UAoA. The trainers hold the view that the Academy is performing well in terms of the number of workshops conducted in a year. It is reported that at least one workshop is being held every month due to the timely availability of funds and expertise from internal as well as external sources. However, some problems are being experienced regarding the category of participants attending a workshop. For instance, workshops intended for senior municipal functionaries (i.e., chairpersons and executive officers) are sometimes attended by the junior functionaries. This happens because many senior functionaries do not give much importance to such initiatives and often direct their subordinate staff to attend the workshops on their behalf. The trainers point out that such practices adversely affect a programme, and will not result in a positive impact of training. To this end, it is emphasised that participation in a workshop should be made compulsory by the state government, irrespective of the fact as to whether the functionary shows interest in attending the workshop.

The participants from Nainital municipal council, on the other hand, are by and large satisfied with the quality of training received from the Academy. In their opinion, their knowledge and understanding of various innovative municipal practices is increasing. Due to this exposure, some initiatives in the form of public-private partnerships have been undertaken in Nainital. However, it is still difficult for them to undertake many other initiatives required for strengthening infrastructure and services due to an acute shortage of funds with the municipal council. The data on revenue generated during the year 2004-05 show that the council mainly relies on external sources of funds, such as the grants recommended by the State Finance Commission (SFC)[8] and other Central/state government grants and bank loans. Together, these account for nearly a half of the total income of the council. On the other hand, income derived from internal sources, such as taxes and non-taxes, is less than 40 per cent of the total income of the council. Furthermore, the amount recovered by the council from citizens on account of sanitation tax, building tax and rent is only 40 per cent of the total demand. The data thus reveal that the financial performance of the council is not satisfactory because generation of revenue from internal sources is too low (Table 3.5). Discussions held with the

8. Local governments receive a consolidated amount every year from the state governments based on State Finance Commission's (SFC) recommendations to fulfill their expenditure responsibilities, including those related to the development and provision of essential urban/municipal/civic services. The Finance Commissions of various states have recommended general principles in respect of fiscal transfers from the states to *panchayats* (i.e., rural local governments) and municipalities. Such fiscal transfers/devolution of funds from the state government to the local governments are distributed among the different categories/types of urban local governments (namely, municipal corporations, municipal councils and town/*nagar panchayats*) on the basis of criteria, such as population size and geographical area. Within this scheme of devolution, emphasis is simultaneously laid on making local government authorities realise that they should make productive use of their own resources by the effective implementation of their tax laws and recovery of their dues.

municipal functionaries also reveal: an acute shortage of funds for implementing infrastructure projects; delays in receiving SFC grant; delays in payment of salaries to staff; vacant positions and shortage of staff that adversely affect the functioning of various sub-committees;[9] lack of computer skills among staff and poor disposal of sewage and solid waste.

Table 3.5

Financial Condition of Nainital Municipal Council, 2004-05

Description of Item	*Status*
Total income; and main sources of income	Rs 57.25 million; SFC and other grants and bank loan (about 50%), building tax (9.61%), conservancy tax (9.61%), motor vehicle fee (8.73%), rent (5.24%).
Percentage of income from taxes to total income of the council; taxes levied	19.34%; tax on buildings, conservancy tax, tax on boats and horses, show tax
Percentage of income from non-taxes to total income of the council and non-taxes levied	18.64%; rent; fee from educational institutions, slaughter houses, projections, library, motor vehicles; stamp duty; licence; etc.
Percentage of income from taxes and non-taxes to total income of the council	37.98%
Total expenditure and departments incurring high expenditure	Rs 57.25 million; Conservancy Department (34%);
	Public Works Department (7%).
Percentage of recovery from sanitation tax, building tax and rent against demand	40.15%

Source: Council budget; tax/non-tax demand and recovery statement of the Council.

9. A municipality is the apex body, which is empowered to constitute various sub-committees. It may delegate all or any of its powers and functions to a sub-committee. Sub-committees are, therefore, constituted for assistance in administrative matters. This helps in the distribution as well as in the speedy implementation of works. The 'Byelaws, Rules and Regulations' of the Nainital Municipality, 1966 provides for the appointment of the following eight sub-committees: (i) finance, toll and taxes; (ii) public works; (iii) assessment; (iv) public health; (v) education; (vi) market; (vii) library and (viii) flats (a place with a flat area adjoining the lake, which is also the venue for various cultural programmes organised by the council). Each sub-committee comprises five to nine members who are elected on the basis of voting among the councillors.

It is pertinent to share the experience of a five-day training workshop on 'Financial Management and Resource Mobilisation' organised by the Academy and attended by Uttarakhand municipal officials (i.e., accountants and engineers). The purpose of the workshop was to raise the awareness levels of participants on the benefits to be achieved from effective financial management, and to inform them about new avenues for mobilisation of funds. It was envisaged that the participants would be in a position to successfully accomplish the following tasks at their place of work upon completion of the workshop: (i) explore options for resource mobilisation, such as improved recovery of property tax and service charges, public-private partnerships, etc., and (ii) amend the accounting rules, audit procedures and budget practices. After the lecture sessions, participants were escorted to the office of Nainital municipal council to learn about new practices adopted by the council for generating additional funds. The practices were first explained and then the participants were taken to the actual site for a personal observation of the initiatives undertaken by the council. The initiatives are briefly described below.

- An important mode of public transport in the plain areas of the town is the cycle rickshaw. To improve this service, the council has tied up with a local private operator and established two cycle rickshaw stands with proper shade facility for the convenience of commuters. The private operator has also played an important role in the arrangement of additional cycle rickshaws and rickshaw pullers. Thus, the private operator recovers charges from the users of this service, and the council earns income by issuing licences to the cycle rickshaw pullers. Furthermore, the council allows private companies to install advertisements displaying consumer products on the rickshaw stand, for which a fee is charged.
- The council has signed a three-year agreement with the Nainital Bank and the Bank of Baroda to install 150 poles for street lighting on the Mall road situated along the lake. The banks took interest in this proposal and offered financial support to the council. Today, they are getting tremendous publicity and response from the people due to advertisements displayed on the street lighting poles regarding various investment schemes and loans. Similarly, the state

Bank of India has placed about 10 dust bins on the busy Mall road. The advertisements of the bank are displayed on the dust bins.

- Nainital is a popular hill resort visited by a large number of domestic and international tourists round the year. Availability of basic civic services to the tourists is, however, a major issue. To address this problem, the council has awarded contracts to local private operators for the construction and maintenance of community toilets in the town. The operators recover the cost from users by levying a nominal service charge. Advertisements of various companies are also installed on the toilet premises for generating income.
- Free entry of vehicles to the Mall road resulted in frequent congestion. To check the traffic jam, the council installed barriers at each entry point of the road and levied a fee. However, due to shortage of staff and non-cooperation by the local/tourist population, the council was unable to manage this activity efficiently. The council has benefitted enormously by contracting out services of fee collection for entry to the Mall road to a private operator. It is reported that when one check-post was contracted, the council earned Rs 3.3 million during a year. After contracting out all three check-posts, the council earned Rs 6.75 million.

Interactions with select elected ward representatives[10] from the Nainital council provide further evidence on the impact of capacity building efforts. It is reported that their knowledge on municipal work practices has improved, and they are able to participate effectively in the municipal decision-making process. Some councillors have acknowledged that they had learned a lot from the training, especially on topics such as 'community mobilisation and resource management in operation and maintenance of services.' It has been instrumental in resolving simple

10. A municipal area is divided into wards in such a manner that the population in each ward is kept the same, as far as possible. Furthermore, the number of wards to be delimited in a municipal area depends on the population of the town. For example, the Haryana Municipal Act, 1973 provides that municipalities with a population size of 100,000–300,000 will have 31 wards. There is a contest for the seat/post of councillor/elected ward representative in municipalities among the eligible voters at the ward level. One person from each ward is elected to the post of councillor.

problems of development at the ward level. For example, in Ward No. 1 of the town, the councillor has coordinated the work of providing footpaths and streetlights by involving the ward residents. Realising that the council did not possess adequate funds and manpower, the residents readily agreed to donate funds for this purpose. Similarly, in Ward No. 3 of the town, the councillor has received active support from the ward residents to carry out a cleanliness drive without the involvement of the council's sanitary workers.

Conclusion

This study makes the point that capacity building is an initiative of genuinely practical worth undertaken by the Central government for improving the efficiency of urban local government institutions. This finding is confirmed from a review of practices adopted by the Uttarakhand Academy of Administration in the conduct of training programmes for municipal functionaries, and the impact of capacity building efforts in Nainital. The study shows that the Academy has taken several steps to ensure that training programmes are conducted effectively and regularly. The following achievement of the Academy needs to be highlighted: it possesses appropriate infrastructure required for the purpose of training; it collaborates with various national and international agencies to obtain financial support and technical expertise; identifies workshop themes in consultation with the participants, giving due consideration to local issues of governance and lays emphasis on interactive class room lectures, documentaries, and field visits for a first hand understanding of the ground realities and the new initiatives carried out by the municipality.

The proactive effects of capacity building initiatives in Nainital were as estimated from the feedback from the participants of the programmes. It is reported that the Academy's approach to training programmes was to create awareness on numerous aspects concerning the efficient functioning of municipalities, about which the participants had been totally ignorant. Due to this exposure, the functionaries have been able to experiment with some innovative practices with appreciable level of success. For example, to improve civic service delivery, the council awarded service contracts to various private and public entities. Such public-private partnerships have also helped in the generation of additional funds. Similarly, some elected ward representatives in Nainital have successfully mobilised funds from the community for providing basic civic services in their wards.

The study has also thrown light on a number of problems, such as attendance by junior municipal functionaries in a training programme intended for senior functionaries, lack of interest among some functionaries in attending programmes, and shortage of funds with the Nainital Council. Such problems adversely affect the whole purpose of the programme and urgently needs to be addressed. At the same time, the Central and state governments should make extra efforts to identify and attend to the growing manpower, equipment, and financial needs of the local government. A visit to the office of the Nainital Council revealed that the municipality is hardly equipped to carry out its duties efficiently. In such situation, only a few lessons learned in the training can be applied by the functionaries.

This study recommends for the following measures with respect to the capacity building initiative of the Indian government:

- Additional training institutions should be established in each Indian state/UT so that all municipal functionaries get the opportunity to attend training programmes at regular intervals; funds for organising programmes should be made available from Central/state government sources, and from other national/international funding agencies. Some existing academic/research institutions in various states may be identified and involved in municipal capacity building.
- All municipal functionaries should be encouraged to attend training programmes regularly. The concerned departments at the state level (such as the Directorate of Local Bodies, etc.) as well as the municipality should maintain time-series data on the number and category of participants by municipality.
- In some cases, arrangements should be made for organising training programmes within the premises of the local government, which will ensure higher participation of the municipal functionaries, and will save travel/accommodation-related costs.

- Select priority areas of training should be identified upon a detailed appraisal of local-level issues and availability of funds, for a greater impact of training and to minimise wastage of resources.
- There should be a proper follow-up of capacity building efforts in respect of each municipality by way of impact assessment.

References

ADB (2009). "Indonesia: Capacity Building in Urban Infrastructure Management Project", Validation Report. Independent Evaluation Department. Available from: *http://www.adb.org/Documents/Reports/Validation/INO/in154-09.pdf*

Aijaz, R. (2007). "Challenges for Urban Local Governments in India", *Asia Research Centre Working Paper* 19. UK: London School of Economics and Political Science.

———. (2008). "Form of Urban Local Government in India", *Journal of Asian and African Studies* 43 (2): 131-154. USA: Sage Publications Ltd.

Amos, F.J.C. (1989). "Strengthening Municipal Government", *Cities* 6 (3): 202-208.

Bontenbal, M.C. (2009). "Strengthening Urban Governance in the South through City-to-City Cooperation: Towards an Analytical Framework", *Habitat International* 33 (2): 181-189.

Hogan, J. (February 2006). "Cambodia, Mongolia, Nepal and Timor Leste Learn from the Udon Thani Cities without Slums Initiative", *UN Habitat Training and Capacity Building Newsletter*.

Ministry of Urban Development (2009). *Newsletter* 1(1). New Delhi: Government of India. January.

———. (2010). *Annual Report 2009-10*. New Delhi: Government of India.

———. (2006a). *Annual Report 2006-07*. New Delhi: Government of India.

———. (2006b). *Report of the Working Group on Urban Development (Excluding Urban Transport), Urban Water Supply and Sanitation (Including Low Cost Sanitation, Sewerage and Solid Waste Management) and Urban Environment for Eleventh Five Year Plan (2007-2012)*. New Delhi: Government of India. Available from: *http://planningcommission.nic.in/aboutus/committee/wrkgrp11/wg11_urbandev.pdf.*

Sharma, K.P. (non dated). *LOGOTRI: Capacity Building through Networking for Effective Local Governments*. Available from: *http://www.bestpractices-search.com/articles/0411281404.pdf.*

Sidabutar, P., N. Rukmana, R.V.D. Hoff and F. Steinberg (1991). "Development of Urban Management Capacities: Training for Integrated Urban Infrastructure Development in Indonesia", *Cities* 8 (2): 142-150.

Tuts, R. (December 2007). "Institutional Building: Five Years of Strengthening Institutions", *UN Habitat Training and Capacity Building Newsletter*.

———. (2006). "Making Learning Matter: Training Impact on Performance", *UN Habitat Training and Capacity Building Newsletter*. February.

UN Habitat (2009). "Training and Capacity Building Activities", Available from: *http://www.unchs.org/list.asp?typeid=13&catid=259&RecsPerPage=ALL*

UNDP (2007). "Fact Sheet, Capacity Building for Decentralised Urban Governance", Available from: *http://data.undp.org.in/factsheets/dg/may07/UrbanGovernance.pdf*

UNESCAP (2009). "Regional and Local Networks: LOGOTRI", Available from: *http://www.unescap.org/pdd/prs/PartnersNetworks/networks.asp*

World Bank (2009). "Municipal Governance and Institution Building", Available from: *http://web.worldbank.org/external/projects/main?pagePK=217672&piPK=95916&theSitePK=40941&menuPK=64140078&category=THEME&goalid=73*

———. (2000). *Cities in Transition: A Strategic View of Urban and Local Government Issues. Executive Summary*. March.

4 e-Governance Initiatives in Municipalities

To keep up with the changing times, governments throughout the world are adopting new technologies to improve work practices. A case in point is electronic governance (henceforth e-Governance). What is e-Governance? Why is it gaining popularity? What steps have been taken by the Indian government to promote this practice at the municipal level? In which activities (or functions/services) are municipalities in different Indian states using this practice? What has been the impact of this initiative, and what are the problems being faced? These are some of the questions which have been discussed in this chapter.

The literature on e-Governance offers a variety of definitions of the concept (Box 4.1). All of these point to the use of a modern communication technology, such as the internet, by the government and its agencies to interact in a convenient and effective manner with various groups and individuals from the government, private sector and the civil society. Of late, municipal governments in India are using technology in various activities to provide information and better services to the urban residents.

Emphasis on e-Governance at the Municipal Level

Increasing emphasis on implementation of e-Governance projects at the level of the municipality is a recent phenomenon. It was made possible in 2003 with the launch of a National e-Governance Plan (NeGP),[1] jointly formulated by the Department of Information Technology (DIT) under the Ministry of Communications & Information Technology (MIT) and the Department of Administrative Reforms and Public Grievances (DARPG) under the Ministry of Personnel, Public Grievances & Pensions (MPPGP).

1. Details on National e-Governance Plan available on website of Department of Information Technology, Government of India.

Box 4.1

Defining e-Government and e-Governance

The terms "e-Government" and "e-Governance" are often used in overlapping manner, although the two are not exactly the same thing. Much of this is due to the lack of a standard definition of e-Governance and we in India have been using this term in a general sense. In the case of e-Government, the services and information are delivered to the citizens or clients through electronic medium, while in the case of e-Governance, the interaction between the citizen and the government takes place through electronic medium and decisions are processed electronically. It is necessarily more interactive and goes beyond e-Government. Electronic governance is, thus, the application of information technology (IT) to the processes of government functioning in order to bring about simple, moral, accountable, responsive and transparent (SMART) governance.

Evolution of e-Governance is a highly complex process requiring hardware, networking, software and re-engineering of the procedures for examination of cases and decision-making. Some of the important pre-requisites for successful e-Governance are: (i) large-scale computerisation; (ii) capability of use of local languages in the IT systems; (iii) changing the mindset of government functionaries; (iv) creation of adequate and appropriate infrastructure; (v) standardisation in data encoding, application logic, user interfaces, etc.; (vi) knowledge networking for better governance; and (vii) creation of public key infrastructure and certification authorities

(Planning Commission, 2001: v).

The plan is an outcome of a series of initiatives announced during the Independence Day celebrations in 2002 by the then Prime Minister of India. The present government approved the plan in May 2006 for implementation at all levels—national, state and local—of the government in phases.

The objective of this initiative is to 'lay the foundation and provide the impetus for long-term growth of e-Governance within the country. The plan seeks to create the right governance and institutional mechanisms, set up the core infrastructure and policies and implement a number of Mission Mode Projects at the Centre, State and integrated service levels to create a citizen-centric and business-centric environment for governance'.[2]

NeGP contains proposals on various projects (Table 4.1), some of which have already been implemented in different parts of the country. Included in the list are a number of Central, state and integrated projects, termed as mission mode projects (MMPs).[3] A national MMP has been identified for implementation in municipalities. The responsibility for the preparation and implementation of this project lies with the Ministry of Urban Development (MoUD).

Table 4.1

Activities and Projects Proposed in the National e-Governance Plan

S. No.	*Activity/Project*	*Brief Activity Details/Coverage*
1	Implementation strategy	Integrated approach; implementation framework
2	Central MMPs	Banking; Central excise and customs; income tax; insurance; Ministry of Company Affairs–MCA21; national citizen database; passport, immigration, visa and foreigners registration and tracking; pension; e-office
3	State MMPs	Agriculture; commercial taxes; e-District; employment exchange; land records; municipalities; *panchayats*; police; road transport; treasuries
4	Integrated MMPs	Common services centre; e-Biz; e-Courts; e-Procurement; electronic data interchange for trade (e-Trade); national e-Governance service delivery gateway; India portal
5	Components	Common services centre; statewide area networks; state data centres
6	Other components	Capacity building; standards; awareness and communication; assessment
7	NeGP programme management unit	Awareness and communication; assessment; capacity building; common services centre; infrastructure and technical; monitoring and evaluation; project finance and appraisal; research and development

Source: Department of Information Technology.

2. Department of Information Technology (DIT), Ministry of Communications and Information Technology, Government of India: *http://mit.gov.in*.

3. 'Mission Mode implies that the objective and scope of the project are clearly defined, that the project has measurable outcomes and service-levels, and the project has well-defined milestones and timelines for implementation' (DIT).

Municipalities have been included in the NeGP to ensure efficiency in the delivery of various services to citizens living in urban areas. Thus, when municipal functions are placed in e-Governance mode, citizens do not have to travel to municipal offices for the services which they require from the municipality. The project for municipalities is considered as one of the components in the Eleventh Five Year Plan (Planning Commission). Since the approval of the National Mission Mode Project (NMMP) for municipalities by the Indian government, the MoUD has initiated the process of implementing the project. The following sub-sections describe the evolution of e-Governance in Indian municipalities.

e-Governance: An Integral Component under JNNURM

To achieve the objectives of the Jawaharlal Nehru National Urban Renewal Mission (JNNURM), state and local governments are being assisted in the implementation of various mandatory reforms, including introduction of a system of e-Governance using information technology applications, such as Geographic Information System (GIS) and Management Information System (MIS) in various services provided by municipalities and other city-level agencies. To ensure that all components under the programme are implemented in a planned manner, necessary guidelines, toolkits, checklists and benchmarks have been prepared to assist Mission stakeholders.[4] It is expected that e-Governance in municipalities will lead to reduced cost and time in service delivery processes.

NMMP: Conceptualisation and Design

To conceptualise, design and implement the project, various e-Governance initiatives already underway in different municipalities of India preceding the launch of NeGP were examined to learn important lessons, including complete functionality requirements. This exercise was undertaken in seven municipalities, namely Hyderabad and Visakhapatnam (Andhra Pradesh), Bengaluru (Karnataka), Kalyan and

---

4. For details visit website of JNNURM: *http://jnnurm.nic.in*; Ministry of Urban Development. *Handbook on Service Level Benchmarks for e-Governance in Municipalities*.

Mumbai (Maharashtra) and Coimbatore and Tiruchirappalli (Tamil Nadu). Pricewaterhouse Coopers (PwC), a private firm, in association with the Financial Institutions Reform and Expansion Programme of the USAID have supported the MoUD in this task. The assessment revealed certain prerequisites for taking up e-Governance as a national-level initiative, such as 'preparing municipalities for fundamental change; re-engineering core business processes; creating integrated data bases and; the capacity to manage information' (Bhattacharjee, 2007).

Available applications of solution providers currently in use in some municipalities were evaluated and benchmarked by standardisation testing quality certification. The purpose was to consider the applications of some qualified application providers. Singh (2007) suggested that, 'this approach will be useful in quickly implementing the initiative, rather than re-inventing the wheel'. Several private firms in India have shown interest in providing technical inputs required for e-Governance to improve internal efficiencies in municipalities as well as service delivery. Oracle's proven packaged/partner solutions are being used in Hyderabad, Kolkata, Uttarakhand municipalities, Kalyan-Dombivli, Ahmedabad, Andhra Pradesh municipalities, among others. Sheshagiri (2007) holds the view that, 'Oracle's experience in deploying the call centre for non-emergency services in the city of New York can be useful for Indian municipalities in terms of integrating "back end" information and allowing a one-stop access of this information to citizens'. Similarly, eGovernments Foundation, in partnership with Infosys, has a mission to provide e-Governance software platform to run city municipalities. The Foundation makes software system available for free to city municipalities in India, although it charges for implementation and customisation services. The products are licence free. eGovernments Foundation has e Governance product suite-municipal systems for various types of municipalities (egov News, 2007a).

NMMP: Coverage, Financing and Implementation

The MMP on e-Governance for municipalities is one of the components under the JNNURM. Initially, the project is being implemented in all the municipalities of 35 cities having population of more than a million as per 2001 census. Subsequently, it will be extended to the remaining town and city municipalities of India. In the first phase of the scheme, the following services are being covered:

- Registration and issue of birth and death certificates.
- Payment of taxes and other utility bills, including property tax, water charges, etc.
- Grievances and suggestions.
- Building plan approvals.
- Procurement and monitoring of projects.
- Health programmes, including licences and solid waste management.
- Accounting system.
- Personnel information system.

The financing of e-Governance projects under JNNURM is based on sharing of costs between the Centre, state and local agencies (Table 4.2). State governments have identified state level nodal agencies (SLNAs) to assist in the implementation of NMMP. The agencies are responsible for preparation of detailed project reports (DPRs), which provide information on cost assessment, scope of various activities, performance levels for each municipality, timelines and milestones of services, and the financial plan. In this endeavour, SLNAs are assisted by consultants. Thereafter, project reports are forwarded to the State Level Steering Committees for approval and submission to the Government of India. At the national level, the National Steering Group provides strategic direction to the implementation of the project. Project proposals received from state governments are processed and placed for appraisal before the Central Sanctioning and Monitoring Committee (CSMC) constituted in the MoUD. Finally, NMMP is implemented at the municipal level through a business model either by public-private partnership (PPP), or by the concerned municipality (MoUD, 2008). Some Indian states that have already accomplished the task of implementing e-Governance projects in select municipalities under the JNNURM include Andhra Pradesh, Gujarat, Karnataka, Maharashtra, Rajasthan, Tamil Nadu, Uttar Pradesh and West Bengal.

Table 4.2

Financing of e-Governance Projects under JNNURM

Category of Cities/Towns/UAs	*Grant*		*ULB or Parastatal Share/ Loan from Financial Institutions*
	Centre	*State*	
Cities/UAs with four million plus population as per 2001 census	35	15	50
Cities/UAs with million plus but less than four million population as per 2001 census	50	20	30

Notes: Figures shown in the table are percentages; UA stands for urban agglomeration.
Source: Website of JNNURM.[5]

Promotion of e-Governance in India

A number of events at the international, national, regional and state level have been organised both independently and jointly by the government and numerous private organisations for widespread promotion of e-Governance in India. In fact, this is an ongoing activity (Box 4.2). It is observed that e-Governance practices have been in existence in some municipalities of the country much before the formulation of NeGP in 2003. The NeGP aims to ensure that it reaches every part of the country.

Use of information and communication technology is quite common in various departments and organisations. The events on e-Governance thus provide an opportunity for the exchange of ideas and for sharing experiences by professionals affiliated with various government departments and private organisations, intellectuals from industry and academic institutions, etc. As a result of the deliberations and recommendations, a number of e-Governance initiatives have been undertaken in various states as well as at the Centre. Recent events on e-Governance also include sessions exclusively on e-Governance in municipalities, wherein experiences in various parts of the country are shared and discussed.

5. Ministry of Urban Development. Guidelines on National Mission Mode Project on e-Governance in Municipalities as part of JNNURM. Available from *http://jnnurm.nic.in/nurmudweb/e-Gov/guidelineegov.pdf*

Box 4.2

Major Events on e-Governance

International Conferences on e-Governance (ICEG)

7th: 22-24 April 2010, Bengaluru, India

6th: 18-20 December 2008, New Delhi, India

5th: 28-30 December 2007, Hyderabad, India

4th: 15-17 December 2006, New Delhi, India

3rd: 9-11 December 2005, Lahore, Pakistan

2nd: 29 November to 1 December 2004, Colombo, Sri Lanka

1st: 18-20 December 2003, New Delhi, India

*National Conferences on e-Governance**

14th: 10-11 February 2011, Aurangabad (Maharashtra): Bronze to Rajkot Municipal Corporation for innovative use of technology.

13th: 18-19 February 2010, Jaipur (Rajasthan): No awards for municipalities.

12th: 12-13 February 2009, Goa: Gold to Ahmedabad Municipal Corporation for 'E-City' Project; Bronze to Nagpur Municipal Corporation for best government website.

11th: 7-8 February 2008, Panchkula (Haryana): Bronze to Surat Municipal Corporation for outstanding performance by City Civic Centres in citizen-centric service delivery.

10th: 2-3 February 2007, Bhopal (Madhya Pradesh): Gold to Kalyan Dombivli Municipal Corporation for outstanding performance by Citizen Facilitation Centres in citizen-centric service delivery.

9th: 2-4 February 2006, Kochi (Kerala): Gold to Hyderabad Municipal Corporation and silver to Vejalpur Municipality for professional excellence in process re-engineering.

8th: 3-5 February 2005, Bhubaneswar (Orissa): Bronze to Pimpri Chinchwad Municipal Corporation for outstanding performance by Citizen Facilitation Centres in citizen-centric service delivery.

7th: 13-15 November 2003, Chennai (Tamil Nadu): Merit Citation Award to Coimbatore Municipal Corporation.

Select events organised by MoUD (GoI), other government and private organisations

- Regional workshop on e-Governance under JNNURM, December 2010.

contd...

...contd...

- Meeting to discuss implementation strategy of NMMP on e-Governance in municipalities under JNNURM, 3 December 2009.
- Session on 'e-Governance in urban local bodies/municipalities', Conflux (now renamed as eGov India) 2005,[6] 17-19 October 2005, New Delhi; 23-25 August 2006, New Delhi; 31 July–3 August 2007, New Delhi.
- Meeting on 'Mission Mode Project on e-Governance in municipalities', with representatives from 35 cities (million plus population), 1 February 2005, New Delhi.
- Meeting of 'representatives of solution providers and members of implementation committee on e-Governance in municipalities', 22 December 2004, New Delhi.
- National seminar on 'e-Governance in Municipalities', 2-3 August 2004, New Delhi.
- Meeting of state representatives on 'National Mission Mode Project on e-Governance', 10 February 2004, New Delhi.

Note: * Sufficient information prior to the 6th National Conference is not available.

Sources: (1) International Congress of E-Government;[7] (2) Department of Administrative Reforms and Public Grievances;[8] (3) Egov India 2006 Secretariat;[9] (4) e-Governance Conference Secretariat.[10]

---

6. Conflux: The e-Government conference is a joint effort by Centre for Science, Development and Media Studies (CSDMS), Government of NCT of Delhi, major departments of Government of India, key academic and civil society organisations and multilateral agencies. The aim of the conference is to provide a knowledge sharing platform and a forum for policymakers, practitioners, industry leaders and academicians for converting e-Government vision into actionable programme. For details, see website of e-Governance Conference Secretariat.
7. International Congress of e-Government (ICEG) is a society for the advancement of knowledge in the discipline of e-governance and promotion of the same in the various levels of governments across the globe. This society was established in 2005 under the aegis of Global Institute of Flexible Systems Management (GIFT) as its Strategic Professional Unit. ICEG serves as a premier global organisation where various stakeholders (i.e., academics, government officers, industry, professionals, NGOs, citizens, government and international agencies) can participate and share ideas and resources for knowledge creation, skill development, networking and spread of e-Governance at various levels. See website of ICEG: *http://www.iceg.net/* .
8. *http://darpg.nic.in/*.
9. Egov India 2006 Secretariat, Centre for Science, Development and Media Studies (CSDMS), *http://www.egovonline.net/*.
10. e-Governance Conference Secretariat: *http://csdms.in/conflux/index.asp*.

A reference may be made to the National Conferences on e-Governance (Box 4.2). The DARPG in collaboration with DIT and the state governments organise a national conference on e-Governance every year. Until now, 14 conferences have been held in various Indian cities—Aurangabad (Maharashtra), Bengaluru (Karnataka), Bhopal (Madhya Pradesh), Bhubaneswar (Orissa), Chandigarh, Chennai (Tamil Nadu), twice in Goa, Hyderabad (Andhra Pradesh) and Jaipur (Rajasthan), Kochi (Kerala) and Panchkula (Haryana). The event includes an awards distribution ceremony for different categories to individuals/organisations who have successfully implemented innovative projects in various sectors. It is noted that except in year 2010, municipalities have always emerged as one of the winners.

e-Governance Initiatives at the Municipal Level

An attempt was made to identify Indian municipalities which are providing online services. This exercise revealed that in most states/UTs of India, at least one municipality is providing online services for the convenience of urban residents. Generally, it is the largest municipality in the state (i.e., municipal corporation) which provides online services; examples of smaller municipalities are rare, namely Mormugao (Goa), Shillong, Agartala, Puducherry, etc. An exception to this pattern is Tamil Nadu, where a large number of municipalities of different sizes offer web-based services. In the case of few states/UTs, such as Manipur, Nagaland, Andaman and Nicobar Islands, municipal websites could not be located on the internet.

On most municipal websites, English language is the medium of communication. There is also an emphasis on the use of local languages. For instance, Agra, Allahabad, Bhopal and Raipur Municipal Corporation websites also provide information in Hindi; Nashik Corporation in Marathi; Cochin and Thiruvananthapuram Corporations in Malayalam and municipalities of Tamil Nadu provide the option of using Tamil; etc.

Municipalities in some states have made alternate arrangements for those urban residents who do not have internet facility at their home/office. To enable their access to the municipal website, several citizen service/

facilitation centres/kiosks/bureaus[11] have been established in different areas of the city, which provide a variety of services to the citizens. Examples of municipalities providing this service are municipal corporations of Delhi, Surat, Hyderabad, Visakhapatnam, etc. Due to this arrangement, citizens do not have to travel to the municipal office in order to avail various services. Furthermore, toll-free helpline telephone numbers are listed on the website to address the queries of citizens.

The number of municipalities providing online services in some states is growing. This is observed from a review of recent publications on the subject. One reason for this is the implementation of e-Governance projects aiming to bring into its ambit all municipalities in a state. Examples are 'Saukaryam' in Andhra Pradesh and 'Lokvani' in Uttar Pradesh.

Thus, while e-Governance at the municipal level is gaining popularity, it is also learnt that the range and level of services provided online varies from municipality to municipality. Some municipalities (namely Surat, Hyderabad, Coimbatore, Kalyan-Dombivli, Pimpri-Chinchwad, etc.) provide a wide range of services, and for their good performance they have even won awards (see Box 4.2). On the other hand, there are others (such as Bhopal), which offer very limited services. Box 4.3 shows an elaborate list of services/functions available online on various municipal websites for the convenience of citizens and municipal functionaries. However, it may be mentioned here that each service/function listed in the box is not available online on every municipal website.

Case Study of e-Governance Initiatives in Delhi

An important objective of this study is to evaluate the impact of e-Governance initiatives at the level of a municipality. The purpose of this exercise is to describe the benefits experienced by municipalities and the citizens using technology, as well as the problems faced by them in the use of such practices. This section of the chapter provides information on the above mentioned two aspects.

11. A popular term currently in use is G2C (Government-to-Citizen) kiosks.

Box 4.3

Municipal Services/Functions/Information Available Online

- Grievance registration and tracking status.
- Payment of dues/taxes/utility bills (such as property tax, water tax/charges, etc.); method of self-assessment/calculation of property tax; application forms.
- Water supply, drainage connection status; application forms.
- Birth/death registration and issue of certificates; application forms.
- Registration of properties; application forms.
- Issue of licences for buildings, shops, vehicles; trade licence payment; application forms.
- Filing building plan application; tracking status of application and monitoring movement of file; approval of plans; fee details; application forms.
- Sanctioning of infrastructure works; update on infrastructure works executed in the city so that citizens can verify works taken up in their wards; monitoring and tracking the execution of works; contractors' access to tenders; application forms.
- E-procurement—electronic information gathering; tendering services.
- Computerised accrual based double entry accounting system to handle high volume financial data accurately—accounting done as and when a transaction happens irrespective of the actual receipt or payment of money.
- Sanitary vehicle tracking system using radio technology (Global Positioning System-GPS), Geographic Information System (GIS), Global System for Mobile Communications (GSM), etc., to monitor movement of vehicles; shows vehicle number, date, time and location.
- Advertisement (hoarding) installation guidelines and yearly, quarterly, monthly fee/rates for installing ordinary/mobile/bus shelter advertisements.
- Status of legal cases filed in various courts where municipality is one of the parties.

Source: Greater Hyderabad Municipal Corporation(*www.ghmc.gov.in*); Hyderabad First[12] Brochure and other municipal websites.

12. Hyderabad First is a Project launched by Municipal Corporation of Hyderabad. Under this project, every municipal service has been made accessible online.

Selection of a suitable case study for the purpose of assessing e-Governance initiatives is not an easy task. As mentioned earlier, there is at least one municipality in almost every state of India providing online services. Also, the range and level of services provided online varies between municipalities. Considering these facts, a large-sized municipality, which has taken significant steps towards the introduction of technology in its functioning, was selected. Delhi, the national capital, is the second largest urban agglomeration[13] of India which recorded a population of 13.78 million and a density of 9,249 persons per sq km in 2001. During the decade 1991-2001, its population growth rate was 46.31 per cent. It is estimated that by the year 2025, the population of Delhi UA will increase to about 30 million (UN, 2009). Delhi is governed by three local government institutions: (i) Municipal Corporation of Delhi (MCD); (ii) New Delhi Municipal Council (NDMC) and (iii) Cantonment Board. MCD is responsible for providing civic services to 97 per cent of Delhi's population and 94 per cent of the area (Table 4.3).

Table 4.3

Population and Area of Delhi, 2001

Population/Area	*Total*	*MCD*	*NDMC*	*Cantonment Board*
Population	13,782,706	13,363,471(96.96)	294,783(2.14)	124,452(0.90)
Area (in sq km)	1,483	1397.29(94.22)	42.74(2.88)	42.97(2.90)

Note: Figures in parenthesis are percentages to total.

Source: Municipal Corporation of Delhi, 2005.

MCD Project on e-Governance

Use of technology (especially internet connection and computers) in the day to day functioning of MCD was insignificant before 2003. At that time, citizens had the option of either visiting the various departments/ offices of MCD located in different parts of the city for availing services, or discussed their problems with the MCD officials/employees over the telephone. In this process a lot of time was spent, and several citizens were also not satisfied with the practice of direct dealing with the officials.

13. An urban agglomeration (UA) is a continuous urban spread constituting a town and its adjoining urban outgrowths or two or more physically contiguous towns together and any adjoining urban outgrowths of such towns.

In 2002, MCD established a Department of Information Technology. This initiative was taken, after it was realised that electronic technology would facilitate smooth and efficient governance. The main objectives of this department are to: (i) formulate, support, implement, monitor and supervise various information technology (IT) projects and (ii) provide technical support in procurement of hardware and software. Furthermore, in this endeavour, MCD decided to involve a consortium of two companies, namely Electronics Corporation of India Limited (ECIL), which is a public sector enterprise under the Department of Atomic Energy, Government of India and SARK Systems India Limited, Hyderabad to implement the project on 'build, own, and operate' (BOO) basis. MCD allowed the companies to recover a nominal transaction fee from the citizens for each transaction that took place on the system. Since the establishment of the IT department of MCD, the following major initiatives have been taken:

- *Formulation of IT Master Plan 2005*: The plan, which was prepared by Tata Consultancy Services (TCS) in 2002-03, gives a holistic view of e-Governance initiatives, such as strategies, project components, timeframe, implementation alternatives and cost estimates. It proposes an investment of Rs 400 million over a period of three years for various departmental applications (Mehta, 2005).
- *Launch of MCD website (www.mcdonline.gov.in)*: The website was launched in February 2003 for the purpose of providing various services online to the citizens of Delhi.[14]
- *Establishment of citizen service bureaus (CSBs)*: Air-conditioned CSBs have been established in different parts/zones of the city for the convenience of those citizens who do not have access to internet facility at their home or place of work. There is also a plan for provision of: (i) one CSB in every municipal ward so that citizens do not have to walk a distance of more than 2-3 kms to avail MCD services and (ii) kiosks at 8,000 sites to facilitate citizens in paying property tax, electricity and water bills, booking of public places for

14. The website was initially managed by the ECIL-SARK consortium. Subsequently, a new website was launched by the commissioner of MCD on June 23, 2009.

organising functions, registration of births and deaths, etc. The bureaus run by ECIL-SARK consortium (a form of PPP) offer a number of services electronically under one roof on payment of a nominal transaction fee. Every day a large number of transactions take place at the CSBs, and some estimates show that MCD has generated considerable revenue since the establishment of CSBs. Mehta (2005) points out that, 'transactions carried out at CSBs offer greater transparency to the citizens, who were earlier paying bribes for getting various services, such as a birth certificate'.

- *Digitisation of records of important departments*: For preserving valuable data and information, MCD has taken steps to digitise records pertaining to births and deaths, factory licences, etc.
- *Conduct of training programmes*: Orientation programmes are conducted to generate awareness among municipal functionaries on the use of computers.
- *Strengthening of IT infrastructure*: MCD has established IT work stations in each zonal office and in the main office located at Town Hall with computer and printing facility, broadband internet for high-speed connectivity. Availability of this facility enables monitoring of transactions carried out at CSBs, printing of reports, payment of bills and pay slips, creation of database and accessing of core applications developed by various vendors, etc.

Services Available on MCD Website and at CSBs

The website and CSBs offer a wide variety of information and services for various categories of users (Table 4.4). For example, citizens can avail the following services online: filing property tax returns; registering and ordering birth and death certificates; ordering and renewal of factory licence; submit tenders for development works; book community halls and parks for private functions, such as marriage parties; download application forms; view list of zones, wards and colonies and download information on various municipal practices.

Table 4.4

Information and Services Available on MCD Website

S. No.	*Category*	*Online Services/Information*
1	Payment of taxes	• File property tax returns and make payment • View arrears of property tax
2	Health	• Register and order birth and death certificates • Search birth and death records • Procedure for registering births and deaths • Procedure for online institutional (i.e., hospitals, nursing homes) registration of births and deaths and application form for health institutions • List of MCD hospitals • Information on dengue, malaria, cholera • Registration of births and deaths Act, 1969 • Information on child immunisation
3	Licence	• Order trade licence • Order factory licence • Order health trade licence; procedure for issue/renewal/amendment
4	Tender	• List and details of tenders invited by MCD from eligible contractors for development of roads, primary schools, etc. • Tender document details (such as toll collection at inter-state border, allotment of kiosks) • Submission of tenders by contractors
5	Community services	• Book community halls • View park availability and book parks • Instructions for booking of parks and community halls
6	Downloadable forms	• Factory (new licence; cancellation, modification) • Trade (new licence) • Affidavits • Property tax (self-assessment)
7	Miscellaneous	• Citizen Geographic Information System (GIS) Portal: view zones, wards, colonies; track new properties • Online registration of shops and establishments • Details of contracts executed by MCD; list of projects above Rs 5 million; works awarded under JNNURM • Status of MLA and councillor fund

contd...

...contd...

S. No.	Category	Online Services/Information
		• Request for proposals (such as underground multi-level car parking, Ghazipur slaughter house) • Expression of interests (such as action plan for solid waste management under Yamuna Action Plan–II) • List of MCD schools • Security guidelines for colony residents • Information on de-silting of drains • Building bye-laws • Duty list of *safai karamcharis*/sweepers

Notes: Grievance registration service,[15] receiving and sanctioning of building plans, GPS to track garbage trucks, currently not available on the MCD website; software for obtaining various types of licences (indicated in the table) is not yet fully developed (as informed by Factory Licensing Department officials on June 25, 2008).[16]

Source: Municipal Corporation of Delhi (*www.mcdonline.gov.in*).

Impact of e-Governance Initiatives

This section provides information on three municipal services which can be accessed by the citizens and functionaries by visiting the MCD website. They are: (i) filing of property tax returns and payment of tax; (ii) registration and issue of birth and death certificates and; (iii) publication, submission and processing of tenders. The scope of each service described includes an appraisal of the role of stakeholders in service provision, procedure to be followed for using online services and the role played by

15. Online public grievances, redressal and monitoring system developed by eGovernments Foundation, Bengaluru was launched in March 2005 with the objective of improving city government responsiveness towards their citizens. The application was designed to: accept complaints from citizens on various services offered by MCD; automatically route complaints to the appropriate MCD department, such as town planning, property tax, legal, IT, horticulture, health, finance and accounts, factory licensing, engineering, electricity, education, veterinary, vigilance, etc.; and allow citizens to track the status of their complaints. Due to some reason, this service is no more available to the citizens on the municipal website. However, the citizens can lodge complaints using other options, information on which is available on the website. For instance, citizens can approach the elected functionaries, such as the Councillors, Mayor and the municipal officials, namely the Additional and Deputy Commissioners and other senior officers, for the redressal of their grievances. They can also contact the Assistant Public Relations officer for any civic complaint. For this purpose, a 24 hours control room has been set up.
16. More recently (in January 2011), steps have been taken to develop the software required for providing various services online, and to integrate the information system of all departments and offices of the civic agency.

technology. Impact assessment of the three services is carried out by analysing suitable indicators (see Table 4.5) that were identified by undertaking a survey of literature, as well as by holding discussions with select municipal employees. Data on the indicators have been obtained from three different departments of MCD, namely property tax, information technology and engineering. In addition, newspaper clippings and information available on the internet has been reviewed to develop a further understanding on the subject.

Filing of Property Tax Returns and Payment of Tax

Urban local governments are responsible for providing basic civic amenities to citizens. The expenditure incurred by them in providing services is recovered by levying various taxes (i.e., property tax, water tax, sewer tax, etc.) and non-taxes (i.e., user charges, licence fees, etc.).

In April 2007, MCD facilitated for property owners the procedure for filing property tax returns and depositing their tax online. The property tax related information available on the website includes:

- Options available to citizens for filing property tax returns: (a) online (i.e., website), (b) at citizen service bureaus and (c) manually at zonal property tax offices.
- Registration of properties by citizens, which is a precondition for filing returns: Citizens are required to complete a registration form in which property details are to be provided, such as ownership, address, building details, i.e., covered area, occupancy, year of construction, etc. The software also calculates the property tax once details of the property are provided.
- Procedure to calculate and file property tax, print copy of tax return, making payments and getting a receipt.
- Options available to citizens for making payments: Cash, cheque/demand draft, credit card etc.

Data collected from property tax department of MCD show that a total of 0.81 million people paid property tax during the year 2007-08 (Table 4.5). Of this total, as many as 27 per cent paid using online services, and the remaining paid manually. The proportion of online users rose to 37 per cent during 2009-10. It is further observed that MCD collected Rs

10.05 billion as property tax in the financial year ending on March 31, 2008.[17] As reported by the Times of India (2008), 'a 27 per cent increase in collection over the previous year was largely due to efficacy of the online property tax system and waiver on the 75 per cent penalty interest'. Payments were made by cash (2%), cheque/demand draft (84%) and credit card (14%).

As per the Economic Times (2007), 'The use of technology in the provision of this service has helped in resolving the earlier problems of complicated property tax forms, calculation of tax, long queues, and congestion at MCD counters'. According to the Hindu (2008), 'The civic agency has also benefited due to online payments received from about 5,000 non-resident Indians, and nearly 20,000 tax payers living in various cities of India, and having properties in Delhi'. A number of problems have, however, been reported which adversely affect the present practice of online filing of tax returns. Notable among these are the frequent upgrading of the online system (Yahoo India News, 2008a), availability of slow online services due to massive rush for filing returns just before the last date (The Tribune, 2008), and dishonoured cheques.[18] Another important issue is the large number of unregistered properties in most cities of India, about which local government agencies do not have sufficient knowledge. This is due to two reasons—non-reporting by property owners to evade tax and deficiencies in the procedure followed by the civic agencies in the enumeration of properties. Due to this reason, several properties continue to remain outside the tax assessment net, and there is considerable loss of income to the municipality. According to one estimate, out of a total of about three million properties in Delhi, only 900,000 property owners (i.e., 30 per cent) are paying the tax. A recent MCD survey further revealed that as many as 4,816 properties have pending dues up to Rs 500,000 each (The Times of India, 2010). The major defaulters according to MCD are residents living in unauthorised/regularised colonies, DDA, DMRC, NDPL and DJB. To address this issue, the civic agency has collaborated with a Hyderabad-based company, namely CE Info Systems Private Ltd. and initiated a GIS-based mapping project to identify all existing properties in

17. There was an increase in the gross collection, which stood at Rs 11.57 billion during 2009-10 (PTI, 2010).

18. Collections worth Rs 382.6 million were lost because 36,362 cheques bounced.

the city to track the defaulters. The GIS portal displays a map of the entire city showing detailed road network, location of 12 zones, 272 wards, 2,311 colonies and numerous blocks. However, information on the number of houses in each block/colony is still not available. The Survey of India[19] is also carrying out a survey of properties in Delhi, which will help MCD in identifying the property tax defaulters. Another step taken by the civic body to maintain a balance between better civic amenities and financial requirements pertains to revision of property tax rates from time to time.

Registration of Births and Deaths and Issue of Certificates

Urban local governments are responsible for registering births and deaths, and issue of certificates. In Delhi, the Health department of MCD is responsible for providing this service. The certificates are required for various purposes—admission of children in school, employment, inheriting the assets of the person who has passed away, etc.

Births and deaths can occur anywhere—in any hospital (i.e., institutional), or at home (i.e., non-institutional). The procedure for registering institutional and non-institutional events is different. In case of institutional events, it is the primary responsibility of the head of the institution to inform MCD about the event that has taken place. This information is filled in an application form that has been prescribed under the law. These forms are freely available in all hospitals (or any zonal office) and are supplied free of cost by MCD. For registering non-institutional events, the law authorises the head of the family or the nearest relative to report the event at the municipal office. This also requires filling up of a form and submitting it to the nearest registration centre established in various parts of the city.

More recently (since 2003), the registration service has been provided on the MCD website. Hence, in Delhi, births and deaths can be registered in two different ways: (a) by the health institutions empanelled under online institutional registration (OLIR) scheme, accessible by logging in to MCD website and (b) personally, at registration centres/CSBs (which also

19. Survey of India is the national survey and mapping organisation of India under the Department of Science and Technology.

provide online service), where registration (for issue of certificate) is free of charge for a period of 21 days of occurrence of an event, after which a late fee is charged.

Birth and death certificates can be obtained from respective hospitals or zonal offices, and the earlier practice of online ordering has been discontinued because many applicants provided fake details to get the documents. For death certificates, citizens can also apply at 11 crematoriums managed by MCD.

Previously, hospitals and nursing home employees undertook a manual recording of births and deaths in record books, which were sent to MCD department by dispatch staff. Now, as many as 400 major hospitals in the city have the facility of providing the details on a birth/death directly due to the availability of online registration system. The hospitals have been issued user identity and password to gain access to the system for the purpose of reporting (or registering) a birth or a death (Figure 4.1).

Figure 4.1

Procedure for Electronic Registration of Births and Deaths, and Issue of Certificates

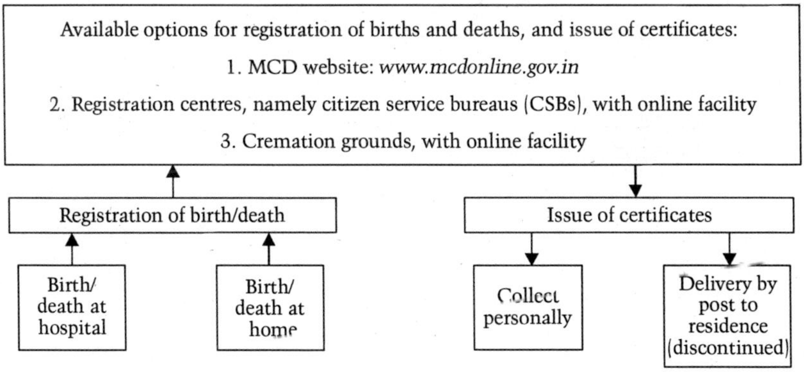

Source: Literature review; discussions held with MCD, ECIL employees, June 2008.

MCD also relies on use of IT in preservation of birth and death records, as well as for searching records maintained in its database. For this purpose, birth and death records have been digitised since 1998 onwards, and certificates are issued immediately in cases where events have occurred during this period. These measures could be taken due to the establishment of a Central Record Room (CRR) in 2005 for storage of all records with proper coding and indexing (The Hindu, 2005), and creation of an online institutional registration system. The computers at CRR have been connected by radio frequency to the health institutions.

In 2004, the civic body received the outstanding performance trophy at the third 'Millennium Plus Cities of India Conference on Registration of Births and Deaths' organised by Registrar General of India at Surat (The Hindu, 2004). It is reported that Delhi has recorded 100 per cent birth and death registration during the past two years, whereas the national average for birth and death registration is 63 and 58 per cent respectively. There is also a plan for replicating the Delhi model of birth/death registration in different states of the country (*expressindia.com*, 2007a).

Information collected from the office of ECIL, which maintains data on transactions taking place at the CSBs, shows that about three to four thousand birth/death certificates were issued in a single day, i.e., on March 31, 2008 and about 0.81 million during one year i.e., 2007-08. Financial data on transactions which took place at CSBs show that during the year 2007-08, an amount of Rs 801.38 million was generated (Table 4.5). The municipal officials hold the view that performance of MCD in the discharge of this duty has improved considerably with the use of technology, including reduced response time and chances of human error.

Citizens earlier applying online often complained about late receipt of birth/death certificates—the certificates being received after a month. In their opinion, work is done much more efficiently at the CSBs, where they get the certificate in about three days time (Yahoo India News, 2008b).

Publication, Submission and Processing of Tenders

Urban local governments invite tender[20] applications from eligible private contractors for undertaking development works, such as construction of roads, drains, overhead water tank, etc. In May 2005, MCD took steps to use technology in the procedures involved in this

20. A tender is a proposal/bid/statement of the price at which one offers to supply goods or services.

process (Figure 4.2) by outsourcing the e-tendering project to Wipro Infotech (egov News, 2007b). In this endeavour, MCD has provided the basic infrastructure in its various offices—computers and internet connections; and Wipro offered the necessary IT support, such as software packages, organisation of training programmes for users and contractors.

The e-tendering software allows MCD officials to post notices on its website for inviting tenders in e-tender format. The notice provides details on: specific department (namely health, engineering, education, conservancy, sanitation, horticulture, information technology, etc.) which has invited the tender; nature of work required to be undertaken, such as development of plots for squatter settlements, construction of underground reservoir, or engagement of security guards/caretakers for providing protection to Slum department assets, etc.; the cost estimates of the work to be undertaken; duration of the project; date of receipt of tender application by the concerned department for purchase of tender by the contractor; date and time for issue, receipt and opening of tender and the guidelines to be followed by contractors in the submission of tenders, such as documents to be enclosed with the application, payment mode, etc.

The MCD e-tendering portal requires registration by contractors to participate in any tendering process, which enables them to access the portal with the help of a user identity and password. For this purpose, a duly completed registration form along with the fee is to be submitted to the concerned MCD department. Registered contractors are also encouraged to participate in a two hour training session conducted twice a week. Training programmes are organised by Wipro, which is the application service provider, for expanding the knowledge of contractors and other users, namely the MCD employees, on the use of the portal, as well as on basic computer operating skills. The e-tendering software allows contractors to prepare and submit their bids (i.e., tender applications) online. It is also mandatory for contractors to possess digital certificates (i.e., signature) for submitting bids against a tender notice, for which they have to apply to a certificate authority, namely SafeScrypt/Tata Consultancy Services. According to the municipal officials, the certificates are tamper-proof and cannot be forged (Box 4.4). MCD employees have also been issued digital certificates to carry out transactions with the contractors.

Box 4.4

A Digital Certificate

According to the Indian Information Technology Act 2000, a digital certificate serves the purpose of a signature for electronic transactions and documents such as bids submitted against a tender. The digital certificate, which is used to digitally "sign" a bid, conclusively proves the identity of the bidder and the authenticity of the bid. Unauthenticated bids are not accepted. Digital certificates allow secure data exchange over the Internet. A digital certificate ensures that the document signed using a certificate has not been tampered with. Digital certificates validate their user's identities, making it nearly impossible to later repudiate a digitally signed transaction

Source: (MCD e-tendering Portal).

Upon receipt of bids from contractors, MCD officials can open/view, compare and process bids using online facility. Public viewing of progress of tenders is also provided for. The time spent in processing each application varies from tender to tender. The final stage in a tendering process is approval of tenders, which is currently done manually (Figure 4.2).

Figure 4.2

Electronic Tendering Process

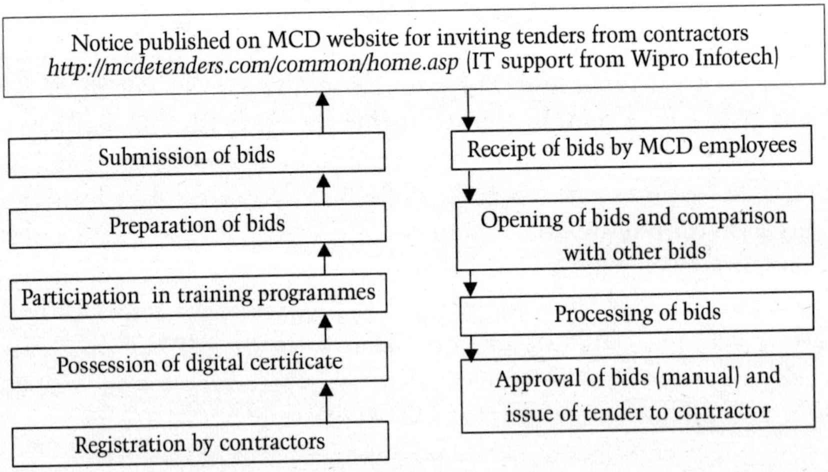

Source: Literature review; discussions held with MCD employees, June 2008.

The use of technology in the tendering process has substantially reduced administrative costs, time, and eliminated difficulties associated with paper work. Previously, contractors had to undertake at least three visits to collect application forms and submit the required documents. In this process, the chances of missing deadlines in the submission of tenders were quite high, because of difficulties posed by physical distance. Furthermore, the number of applications received by MCD from contractors was much less due to several reasons—pressure created by influential contractors, physical distance, etc. Nowadays, all tenders are invited through e-tendering facility by the different MCD departments. As mentioned earlier, contractors can now electronically download and upload tender documents, track the status of tenders and receive e-mail alerts. They can be sure of privacy and confidentiality of their tender proposals. However, all payments are done manually, i.e., by demand draft or cheque because internet payment gateway facility is currently not available. Statistics show that during the three-year period (i.e., 1 April 2005 to 31 March 2008), over 50,000 tenders have been processed online (Table 4.5).

Some problems have been observed in the e-tendering system introduced by MCD. It is reported that only part of e-tendering process is fully automated. Currently contractors can prepare and submit bids and tenders can be opened and processed online, but the process of tender approvals and payments is still manual. The process is time consuming.

Conclusion

Local government institutions in urban areas provide numerous services to the citizens. Several citizens are, however, dissatisfied with the quality of services provided. They feel that a lot of time and money is spent in visiting different departments of the civic agency over and over again for getting simple things done. This is due to numerous problems which they experience during their visit to the municipal office, such as lack of cooperation from municipal employees, congestion, corruption, etc. (Table 4.6).

To address such basic issues of governance being experienced in almost every government department, the Indian government formulated a National e-Governance Plan in the year 2003. The plan provides for the implementation of a number of mission mode projects, including one for municipalities, namely National Mission Mode Project on e-Governance in municipalities. The main objective in this endeavour is to set up the necessary infrastructure (i.e., hardware and software) in municipalities and to enable municipal functionaries to use technology in their day to day activities. The responsibility for the preparation and implementation of this project lies with the Ministry of Urban Development, which has already taken steps in this direction. To ensure its success, promotion of e-Governance at the municipal level is identified as one of the mandatory reforms to be implemented under the Jawaharlal Nehru National Urban Renewal Mission, which is a major urban development scheme launched by GoI in December 2005. Furthermore, numerous conferences and seminars have been conducted on this topic at different places in the country, where professionals from various government departments, private organisations, intellectuals from industry and academic institutions share their ideas and experiences.

With increasing emphasis on the use of technology in governance, websites for a number of municipalities in India have been developed for disseminating information on their activities and practices, as well as for delivering online (i.e., internet-based) services to the citizens, such as filing property tax returns and making payments; registering births and deaths and obtaining certificates; ordering and renewing trade/factory licence; submission and processing of tenders for development works; booking of community halls and parks for private functions, such as marriage parties; downloading various types of forms and registration of shops and establishments. It is learnt that: (i) in most states/UTs of India, at least one municipality is providing online services and usually it is the largest municipality (smaller ones rarely do so); (ii) most municipal websites use English as a medium of communication, though there is also an emphasis on the use of local languages; (iii) municipalities in some states have opened several citizen service centres (offering internet services) in various parts of the city for those residents who do not have internet facility at their home/office and (iv) the range and level of services provided online varies from municipality to municipality. Some municipalities provide a wide range of services, while others offer very limited services. It is also observed that a large number of municipalities in India are yet to take the initiative of using technology in service provision, since it involves technical (i.e., hardware, software and networking) and managerial (i.e., reducing bureaucratic practices, capacity building, etc.) reforms at the municipal level.

An appraisal of the MCD's project on e-Governance confirms the positive role played by technology in the delivery of basic civic services. To determine this fact, suitable indicators (Table 4.5) of the following three services were analysed: (i) filing of property tax returns and payment of tax; (ii) registration and issue of birth and death certificates and (iii) publication, submission and processing of tenders for undertaking construction works. The data show that internet-based services led to a

Table 4.5

Performance of MCD in the Delivery of Online Services

S. No.	*Category*	*Indicator*	*Statistics*	*Date/Period*
1.	Property tax	• Per cent increase in property tax collection during 2006-07 and 2007-08 (%)	27.13	9 April 2008
		• Number of people who paid property tax (in million)	• 0.71 • 0.81 • 0.86 • 0.97	• 2006-07 • 2007-08 • 2008-09 • 2009-10
		• Number of taxpayers who paid using online system (in million)	• 0.19 • 0.22 • 0.33 • 0.37	• 2006-07 • 2007-08 • 2008-09 • 2009-10
2.	Birth and death certificates	• Total number of transactions at citizen service bureaus (CSBs)	in one day: 2,068 in one year: 665,978	• 31 March 2008 • 1 April 2007 to 31 March 2008
		• Total number of certificates issued at CSBs	in one day: 3,630 in one year: 810,772	• 31 March 2008 • 1 April 2007 to 31 March 2008
		• Total amount collected at CSBs (in million Rs)	in one day: 1.17 in one year: 801.38	• 31 March 2008 • 1 April 2007 to 31 March 2008
3.	Tender	• Total number of tenders processed online	Approx. 50,000	1 April 2005 to 31 March 2008

Sources: (a) For property tax – (i) The Times of India, 2008; PTI, 2010; (ii) Property tax collection report of MCD, generated on June 9, 2008; (b) For birth and death certificates – CSB transaction statistics maintained by ECIL office; (c) For tenders – Executive Engineer (Civil), MCD.

huge rise in revenue generated because of the phenomenal increase in the number of:

- payments of property tax,
- birth and death certificates issued,
- tenders processed,

The private sector played an important role in the MCD project on e-Governance, thus illustrating the advantages of public-private partnership. There are several examples. Tata Consultancy Services (TCS) formulated the IT Master Plan for MCD. The ECIL-SARK consortium helped in the implementation of the project on 'build-own-operate' (BOO) basis and also runs citizen service bureaus (CSBs) in different parts of the city and manages the data. It had also prepared the software for birth and death-related services. Votivesoft Business Solutions Private Ltd., a Hyderabad-based IT consulting and services company had designed and deployed the software for providing property tax-related services. CE Info Systems, Hyderabad is preparing a GIS-based mapping project to identify all existing properties in the city. Wipro Infotech has offered technical support in designing software for tender-related services and conducts training programmes for the benefit of municipal functionaries and contractors. SafeScrypt/TCS provide digital certificates (i.e., signatures) to enable MCD employees and contractors to exchange tender-related documents. In the year 2011, Tech Mahindra Ltd. has been involved to build, operate and maintain the ICT-based platform and train the MCD staff before transferring the system to the civic body after five years.

The MCD case study also demonstrates that internet-based services are a basic necessity, especially for large city governments with increasing urban population. By adopting technology in the day to day work, a far larger number of people are served with greater convenience and reliability. The advantages of using internet-based services are listed in Table 4.6.

In any attempt to bring about an improvement in government practices, a number of problems are experienced. In the beginning, the citizens are hesitant because it takes time to get accustomed to new practices, mainly because they do not know about the advantages that new technologies offer. In this situation, it is the responsibility of the civic agency (i.e., the municipal employees and elected representatives) to

Table 4.6

Comparison of MCD Practices in the Delivery of Municipal Services

Old Practice (Manual)	*New Practice (Online/Internet-based)*
• Property tax: Citizens had to visit MCD offices/departments at various locations in Delhi; long queues; complicated tax forms; little cooperation received from officials/staff	• Citizens now have the facility of online services—internet at home/office and citizen service bureaus (CSBs) in different parts of the city; response time, chances of error, paper work and harassment reduced considerably
• Assessment of properties: MCD suffered huge losses due to under assessment of properties. In 2005, estimated number of properties in Delhi were 2.5 million, however, this figure was under assessed by 40 per cent	• Online payments received from NRIs and tax payers living in other cities but having property in Delhi • Newly created geographic information system (GIS) will help in tracking all properties
• Finance: Considerable loss of revenue since adequate facilities were not available to citizens for payment of various taxes and fees	• Significant increase in income of MCD due to online services available to the citizens for the deposit of taxes and fees
• Awareness and time: Many citizens did not know where to get information on various services; depositing bills was time consuming	• Website offers detailed information on procedures citizens need to follow; service delivery is fast and convenient
• Birth and death certificates: Hospitals and nursing homes used to send records of births and deaths in record books through dispatchers; citizens had to pay bribe for getting certificates	• Health institutions enter details directly on the website; procedure made easy and less time consuming; certificates obtained for a nominal fee and within a few days
• Tendering: Contractors had to undertake at least three visits to collect application forms and submit the required documents.	• All tenders are invited using e-tendering facility by the different MCD departments. Contractors can now electronically download and upload tender documents, track the status of tenders and receive e-mail alerts.
• Number of applications received by MCD from contractors was much less due to several reasons—pressure created by influential contractors, physical distance, etc.	• There is a drastic increase in the number of transactions.

Source: Literature survey; discussions held with MCD employees and elected municipal representatives, May-July 2008.

generate awareness among the residents. This problem also exists because of a severe shortage in the number of CSBs/kiosks in the city. Field visits to different parts of the city revealed that there are many citizens who are not aware of the existence of such facilities at all. The MCD plans to set up 8,000 kiosks in the city. Some of the problems reported by the stakeholders require immediate attention. First is the MCD's paucity of funds for implementing the IT master plan. It has a budget of Rs 10 million, whereas the TCS has estimated it would cost Rs 4,000 million (*expressindia.com*, 2007b). Second, the frequency with which the online services need to be upgraded affects work efficiency. Third, some government departments do not yet have automated services (not all departments have been computerised so far) and some others only have partially automated services (only part of e-tendering process is automated). Fourth, there are delays in receiving services, with citizens applying online often complaining about late receipt of certificates. It has been a common grudge of the citizens that the MCD employees are not quick to respond to their complaints. There is meagre information on the website regarding decisions taken on the implementation of infrastructure projects. Then, there is the hesitation among the users to make online payments and finally the recovery from property tax is very low due to the non-availability of data on the total number of properties in Delhi.

To conclude, the future of Indian cities will be shaped by the nature of policies the government formulates and the steps it takes for their effective implementation. In this context, good urban governance practices, such as e-Governance initiatives, should be increasingly adopted by city governments to achieve the vision of fully sustainable cities. Some of the operational problems experienced in the use of technology in service provision, and the high levels of investment required for implementation of e-Governance projects throughout the country are areas of concern. To this end, this study recommends for the following:

- Hardware and (user-friendly) software requirements of municipalities should be fully addressed; supply of electricity in municipal offices should be improved.
- Municipal functionaries should be well trained in the use of computers and software.
- Awareness programmes should be conducted for citizens on the advantages of using new technologies.
- Additional citizen service bureaus should be established for providing electronic services.
- Municipalities should build up a good reputation in the operation and maintenance of electronic services, especially in terms of addressing the complaints of citizens.

References

Bhattacharjee, Nabroon (2007). "Building Sound Local e-Government", Interview, published online in egov magazine, October 8.

egov News (2007a). "e-Governance in Urban Local Bodies: Municipal e-Governance", Session Report, published online in egov magazine.

———. (2007b). "Delhi, India to set up a Comprehensive e-Procurement System", by Kunal N. Talgeri, published online, September 2.

expressindia.com. (2007a). "MCD's Success Story Finally Registers, Online Model set to be Downloaded Across India", September 20.

———. (2007b). "4 Years, 3 Guides and Lakhs Later, MCD Revives Scheme to Make All Files Digital", by Aanchal Bansal, November 17.

Mehta, Rakesh (2005). "Tete-e-tete with MCD Commissioner", Interview, published online in egov magazine, September 9.

Ministry of Urban Development (2008). *Annual Report 2007-08*. New Delhi: Government of India.

Municipal Corporation of Delhi (2005): *Civic Guide*. Delhi: Press and Information Office, Town Hall.

Planning Commission (2001). *Report of the Working Group on Convergence and e-Governance for the Tenth Five Year Plan* (2002-2007). New Delhi: Government of India.

———. *Draft Report of the Steering Committee on Urban Development for Eleventh Five Year Plan (2007-2012)*. New Delhi: Government of India.

Press Trust of India (2010). *All-Time High Gross Property Tax Collection for MCD*. April 8.

Singh, S.P. (2007). "Towards Efficient and Effective Municipal Services", Interview, published online in egov magazine, October 7.

Sheshagiri, A.M. (2007). "Municipal e-Governance Market Opening up in India", Interview, published online in egov magazine, October 8.

The Economic Times (2007). "Pay Property Tax at Click of a Mouse", by Ambika Pandit, April 1.

The Hindu (2008). "MCD Receives Online Property Tax Payment from 97 Countries", July 5.

———. (2005). "Birth and Death Certificates Online", May 8.

———. (2004). "MCD Carves a Niche in Online Registration of Births, Deaths", by Lalit K. Jha, March 5.

The Times of India (2010). "Over 10 Lakh More Properties In MCD Tax Net this Year: Warns of Strict Action Against Defaulters", 17 August.

———. (2008). "MCD Rakes in Rs. 1,000 Crore in Property Tax", April 9.

The Tribune (2008). "MCD e-System to Deposit Property Tax Fails", June 10.

United Nations (2009). *World Urbanisation Prospects: The 2009 Revision*. Department of Economic and Social Affairs, Population Division.

Yahoo India News (2008a). "MCD's Online Property Tax Window Out of Order", April 11.

———. (2008b). "Civic Body's Online Birth Registration Scheme a Flop", May 26.

5 Strengthening Municipal Finance

There is a heavy burden of demands for civic services in Indian cities due to a high concentration of population. Most city governments fail to provide the desired levels of infrastructure and services to the residents both because of the weak financial base and poor financial management. It is a well known fact that income generated by most of the local governments is insignificant and thus there continues to be a heavy reliance on Central and state government funds. At the national level, the Ministry of Urban Development has reported an investment requirement of Rs 8,000 billion for scaling up infrastructure in all the 5,161 Indian towns and cities (MoUD, 2009). Similarly, the Planning Commission/ concerned ministries provide the following estimates of funds required for the upgrading of various sectors during the Eleventh Five Year Plan period (2007-2012): (a) Rs 1,292.37 billion for urban basic services (namely water supply, sewerage and sewage treatment, drainage, solid waste management, etc.); (b) Rs 3,613.18 billion for housing; (c) Rs 768.96 billion for operation and maintenance of various civic services in urban areas during the period 2005-2010 and (d) Rs 1,325.90 billion for urban transport (Planning Commission, Eleventh Five Year Plan, 2007-2012).

This chapter contains information on significant initiatives undertaken to strengthen the financial base of municipalities in India. It begins with a brief description of municipal income and expenditure heads and the financial problems of municipalities. Thereafter, important policy measures initiated by the Indian government are explained. Finally, information collected from a case study, namely Kolkata, is evaluated to assess the performance of the local government in the light of recent financial reforms.

Items of Municipal Income and Expenditure

An in-depth understanding on the various items of municipal income and expenditure can be obtained through a review of the municipal budget.[1] The budget is basically a financial statement of the anticipated income and expenditure prepared annually by each municipality. It is finalised by the functionaries during municipal meetings and thereafter sent for approval to the State government authorities. The various income heads to be included in a municipal budget are determined by the provisions outlined in the municipal act passed by the state legislature, which defines the financial powers of the municipality, including the taxes which it may impose to recover the costs incurred in the provision of civic services.

The budget shows the income the municipality obtains from various internal and external sources, which besides taxes,[2] are: revenues from municipal utilities; duties;[3] licence and various other fees;[4] cess;[5] rent from municipal properties; fines and penalties; fees for services rendered; share in state taxes;[6] government grants/grants-in-aid for general and specific purposes; interest on loan; dividend on investments; loans received; income from sale of assets; recoveries of loans and sale of securities, etc. Expenditure incurred by municipalities is on administration (including staff salaries and allowances); maintenance of roads, buildings, parks, gardens and other assets; social services such as education, medical and public health, water supply and sanitation, etc.

1. 'It means quantitative plan of activities and programs expressed in terms of money in respect of assets, liabilities, revenues and expenses. The budget expresses the ULB goals in terms of specific financial and operating objectives' (MoUD, 2004).
2. Examples of taxes levied by a municipality are property/house tax, water tax, sewer tax, advertisement tax, tax on animals, etc.
3. Stamp duty is imposed whenever urban property is registered or transferred. The basis of the duty is the value of the property as stated in the registration deed.
4. Licence fees are levied on hotels, restaurants and eating places, dairies, workshops and factory premises, sanctioning plans for buildings, etc.
5. Cess is used as rider to a tax for collecting additional revenue for a specific purpose. For instance, there is the education cess, which is paid along with service tax or income.
6. State governments share some taxes (namely entertainment tax, motor vehicle tax) with the local governments. These taxes are collected by the state government and a share is transferred to the local bodies.

Financial Problems of Municipalities

Most municipalities in India do not have sufficient funds at their disposal to carry out duties efficiently which has had a crippling effect on the functioning of vital civic services. This problem has been noted by the Planning Commission, and the various Central committees and commissions constituted from 1870s onwards to examine the functioning of local government institutions (Box 5.1). From a study of reports (Finance Commission, 2004), the following problems can be listed: (i) municipal bodies were subject to the control of the government in so far as no new tax was allowed to be imposed, nor loans allowed to be raised, no work costing more than a prescribed sum undertaken, no serious departure from the sanctioned budget made without previous sanction of the government, and no rules or bye-laws could be enforced without similar sanction; (ii) resources of local bodies were not adequate for the effective execution of the duties assigned to them; (iii) elected members were reluctant to impose or increase local taxes, especially the house, water and conservancy taxes, as any such new burden would fall directly on the electorate; (iv) there was discrimination in the assessment of taxes and inefficiency in their collection, complete disregard for budgetary principles and defective budgeting; diversion of government grants for specific purposes, corruption and embezzlement; (v) while municipal functions were enlarged, financial powers were actually curtailed; (vi) state governments utilised purely local taxes for their own purposes; (vii) local bodies became increasingly dependent on grants-in-aid from state governments which further tightened their grip over the local governments; (viii) in the absence of a clear cut demarcation between state and local sources of taxation, there was encroachment by the state government in the legitimate domain of local taxes; (ix) due to weak financial administration, local authorities failed to meet their obligations; (x) no attempt was made to consider the finances of local bodies as a part of the overall public expenditure of the country; (xi) audit objections remained pending for many years and audit was not conducted regularly in some municipalities; (xii) there was violation in the execution of accounting rules and regulations; (xiii) municipalities were granted limited borrowing powers; (xiv) the local bodies' own revenues were not enough to meet even the operational and maintenance expenditure, and in the case of smaller ULB's, the weak financial position is also combined with the lack of organisational and technical capabilities (some of their functions have been transferred to state-level bodies); (xv) incomplete devolution of functions and funds to ULBs; (xvi) adherence to outmoded methods of property tax assessment and collection, and reluctance to levy user charges; (xvii) state governments continued to take decisions on such matters as rates of user charges, property tax, octroi, role of parastatals in water supply and sanitation services, etc., with little

Box 5.1

Committees and Commissions Constituted to Study the Functioning of Municipalities and Other Legal Initiatives

- Lord Mayo's Resolution, 1870
- Lord Ripon's Resolution, 1882
- Royal Commission on Decentralisation, 1907-08
- Government of India Resolution, 1915
- Government of India Reforms, 1919
- Indian Taxation Enquiry Committee, 1925
- Simon Commission, 1930
- Government of India Act, 1935
- Local Finance Enquiry Committee, 1949
- Taxation Enquiry Commission, 1953
- Central Council of Local Self Government, 1954
- Committee of Ministers for Local Self Government, 1962
- Rural-Urban Relationship Committee, 1963
- Committee on Training of Municipal Employees, 1963
- Committee on Service Conditions of Municipal Employees, 1965
- Administrative Reforms Commission, 1967
- Committee on Budgetary Reforms in Municipal Administration, 1974
- National Commission on Urbanisation, 1985
- State Finance Commissions, constituted by a provision of Constitution (74th Amendment) Act, 1992

Source: Government of India, 1963 and literature survey.

reference to the ULBs that are affected by these decisions; (xviii) inefficiency in revenue collection, leakage of funds, and violation of fundamental financial principles; (xix) municipalities had neither the responsibility nor the autonomy of fiscal powers for delivering the urban services expected from them; there was a mismatch between municipal revenue capacities and their financial requirement; (xx) the accepted State Finance Commission (2005-2010) (SFC) recommendations were not fully implemented due to resource constraints; (xxi) most SFC reports did not contain an estimation and analysis of the state governments' or the local bodies' finances at the pre- and post-transfer stages along with a quantification of the revenues that could be generated additionally by the local bodies, making it impossible for the Twelfth Finance Commission (2005-2010) to give recommendations on the states' resource needs based on information contained in the SFC reports; (xxii) there were delays in the constitution of SFCs, often carried out in phases and frequently reconstituted, there were issues related to qualification of members chosen, delayed submission of reports and delayed tabling of the action taken report in the legislature, which all add up to defeating the very purpose of this institution; (xxiii) Central government grants released to states took a long time to reach local bodies.

Government Policy Initiatives to Strengthen Municipal Finance

Given the dire condition of their finances, local governments cannot be expected to meet their requirements from traditional sources alone, and thus, the only option left is to develop novel ways for overcoming the present shortage. With this realisation, several innovative efforts to strengthen municipal finance have been initiated at various points of time. A brief description of the significant initiatives as well as the problems experienced in implementation is presented in this section.

Central Finance Commission

The institution of Finance Commission is appointed every five years under Article 280 of the Indian Constitution. It was conceived for the purpose of recommending the transfer of a part of the excess revenue at the disposal of the Central government to the state governments so as to reduce the growing fiscal imbalances. The First Finance Commission was constituted on November 22, 1951 and its recommendations covered the period from April 1, 1952 to March 31, 1957. The Thirteenth Finance Commission, appointed on November 13, 2007, covers the period between April 1, 2010 to March 31, 2015. The terms of reference of the Thirteenth Finance Commission (2007) are to make recommendations on the: '(i) distribution of the net proceeds of the taxes between the Union and the States and the allocation between the States of the respective share of such proceeds; (ii) principles which should govern the grants-in-aid of the revenues of the States out of the Consolidated Fund of India and the sums to be paid to the States which are in need of assistance by way of grants-in-aid of their revenues and; (iii) measures needed to augment the Consolidated Fund of a State to supplement the resources of *Panchayats* and Municipalities in the State[s] on the basis of recommendations made by the Finance Commissions of the State[s]'.

The Finance Commission recommends grants for rural and urban local governments every five years, to be released through state governments at one year interval to enable the local governments to discharge at least their primary functions in an effective manner, including the provision and maintenance of basic civic services, such as primary education, primary health care, safe drinking water, street lighting, sanitation including drainage and scavenging facilities, etc. The Twelfth Finance Commission had recommended grants-in-aid of Rs 50 billion for municipalities for the period 2005-2010 with the objective of improving the standards of civic services. The allocation of these grants among the 28 Indian states is based on fixed criteria and weightage is given to each criterion, they being population (40%),[7] geographical area (10%),[8] distance

7. Population was considered an important factor in determining the needs of the states, in view of the fact that people were affected by the quantity and quality of services. Forty per cent of the amount was allocated to the states to be given to *panchayats* and municipalities on the basis of rural/urban population of the state.

8. Ten per cent of the grant was distributed on the basis of the geographical area of each state. In this case, consideration was given to the fact that the cost of providing basic services in sparsely populated areas is relatively high, and would necessitate giving weight to the expanse of the states.

from the highest per capita income (20%),[9] index of deprivation (10%),[10] and revenue effort (20%).[11] In addition, the Commission recommended a number of measures which could be adopted by the Centre/state governments/local bodies. They were: promotion of public-private partnerships (PPPs) in solid waste management; preparation of comprehensive schemes on composting and waste to energy programmes; creation of database and proper accounting system through the use of modern technology to assess the gap between the cost of service delivery and capacity to raise resources; release of grants-in-aid to a state after it certifies that the previous releases have been passed on to local bodies, which should be done within 15 days from the date of release of the Central grants (Finance Commission, 2004).

Based upon a thorough review of the problems experienced in the past including the conditionalities imposed for release of funds,[12] slow progress in maintenance and auditing of ULBs' accounts, and non-performance by state governments observed from failure in drawing significant proportion of the amount meant for ULBs,[13] the Thirteenth Finance Commission felt the need to adopt a different strategy for devolution (Box 5.2).[14]

---

9. Finance commission used average per capita gross state domestic product (GSDP) excluding primary sector at comparable prices on the basis of GSDP data supplied by Central Statistical Organisation (CSO) and population figures interpolated/projected for three years, *viz.*, 1999-2000, 2000-01, 2001-02 based on 1991 and 2001 Census data on urban population. The distance of each state was measured from the state with the highest average per capita GSDP, plus half of the standard deviation. The distances were then weighted by the urban population for the year 2001 of the respective state to arrive at its share.

10. An index of deprivation was constructed to take into account intra-state disparities on the basis of data relating to certain minimum needs (such as drinking water and sanitation) of the population. The distance from the minimum deprived state was then weighted by the Census 2001 population for rural and urban areas to derive the state-wise share.

11 The commission linked the ratio of the own revenues of local bodies to the state's own revenue and the GSDP separately and assigned a 10 per cent weight to each. The period taken was 2000-01 to 2002-03 in the case of own revenues of local bodies related to states' own revenue and 1999-2000 to 2001-02 in case of own revenues of local bodies related to SDP.

12. At least 50 per cent of the grants provided to each state for urban local bodies (ULBs) should be earmarked for solid waste management through PPP.

13. Under the Twelfth Finance Commission award, 10.57 per cent of eligible allocations for ULBs had not been drawn until 6 November 2009.

14. Report of the thirteenth Finance Commission (2010-15), Chapter 10, Local bodies.

Box 5.2

Grants to Local Bodies Recommended by the Thirteenth Finance Commission of India

Local bodies be transferred a percentage of the divisible pool of taxes (over and above the share of the states) after converting this share to grant-in-aid. The value of the grant must be commensurable at the start of the year, since the grant would have to be included in the Union Budget. The volume of the divisible pool for the previous year be used as a basis for computing the grant eligibility of local bodies for a particular year. For example, the grants-in-aid for local bodies in 2010-11 would be based on a percentage of the divisible pool of 2009-10 (Revised Estimates). After the 'actuals' of that year are determined, adjustments may be made in the second tranche of the two-tranche system. The proposal is to award 2.28 per cent of the relevant divisible pool as a grant to local bodies. This works out to Rs 875.19 billion. Of this total aggregate grant to local bodies, Rs 630.51 billion is meant for rural local bodies, Rs 231.11 billion is for urban local bodies (ULBs), and Rs 13.57 billion is for special areas.

The grant will have two components—a basic component and a performance-based component. The basic grant will be equivalent to 1.50 per cent of the previous year's divisible pool. All states will have access to this grant for all the five years as per the defined criteria and weights. The performance grant—effective from 2011-12—will be 0.50 per cent for the year 2011-12 and 1 per cent thereafter, up to 2014-15. Only those states which meet the stipulations will have access to the performance grant.

An amount of Rs 20 per capita per year has been allocated as the 'special area basic grant' to specially support areas covered by the V and VI Schedules and the areas exempted from the purview of Part IX and IX A of the Constitution. This special area basic grant will be accessible by all the eligible states for all five years. A special areas performance grant of Rs 10 per capita for 2011-12 and Rs 20 per capita for the subsequent three years will be made available to those states which meet the stipulations.

The general basic grant and the total special areas grant has been estimated as aggregating to Rs 576.93 billion for the five-year period 2010-2015. Rs 13.57 billion has been allocated to the special areas grant. This amount represents 2.35 per cent of the basic grant for the

contd...

...contd...

local bodies. This leaves Rs 563.35 billion as the general basic grant to be divided amongst states. The general basic grant and the general performance grant will initially be segmented into rural and urban shares on the basis of their respective populations as per the 2001 Census, with 26.82 per cent as the urban share and 73.18 per cent as the rural share. By thus splitting the total grant provision, a uniform per capita entitlement in both sectors of the economy is provided for. The grant for rural and urban local bodies (ULBs) will then be separately allocated amongst states. However, the special areas grants, both general and performance, will be distributed without distinguishing between urban and rural areas.

The state-wise percentage share of the basic grant to be transferred to ULBs will be based on the following criteria and weights allotted: population (50%), area (10%), distance from highest per capita sectoral income (20%), index of devolution based on amounts devolved to local bodies (15%), and finance commission local body grants utilisation index based on grants awarded by Twelfth Finance Commission and releases made to state governments (5%).

A state government will be eligible to draw its share of the general performance grant only if it complies with the following conditions: it should submit the relevant supplement to the budget documents and certify that the accounting and audit systems have been introduced in all local bodies; a system of independent local body ombudsmen who will look into complaints of corruption and maladministration against the functionaries of local bodies, both elected members and officials, and recommend suitable action is put in place; a system to electronically transfer local body grants provided by this commission to the respective local bodies within five days of their receipt from the Central government is put in place; prescribe through an Act the qualifications of persons eligible for appointment as members of the SFC; local bodies should be fully enabled to levy property tax (including tax for all types of residential and commercial properties); a State-level Property Tax Board, which will assist all municipalities and municipal corporations in the state to put in place an independent and transparent procedure for assessing property tax to be constituted; standards for delivery of all essential services provided by local bodies to be defined; all municipal corporations with a population of more than 1 million (2001 Census) must put in place a fire hazard response and mitigation plan for their respective jurisdictions.

Source: *Report of the Thirteenth Finance Commission (2010-15).*

State Finance Commissions

The efforts of previous committees and commissions to strengthen Indian municipalities finally led to the legislation of the 74th Constitution Amendment Act in 1992. Prior to this, the Constitution did not contain any exclusive provisions for municipal institutions, which were thus subject to the control of the state governments. The 74th Amendment contains a number of provisions, among them being the constitution of state finance commissions (SFC) every five years to review the financial position of municipalities, and make recommendations on the measures needed to improve their financial position (Box 5.3).

Box 5.3

Constitution of State Finance Commission

Articles 243–I and 243–Y of the Indian Constitution allow State governments to constitute a State Finance Commission once in five years 'to review the financial position of the municipalities and make recommendations to the Governor as to –

(a) the principles which should govern -

- (i) the distribution between the State and the municipalities of the net proceeds of the taxes, duties, tolls and fees leviable by the State, which may be divided between them, as also the allocation of the shares of such proceeds between the municipalities at all levels;
- (ii) the determination of the taxes, duties, tolls and fees which may be assigned to, or appropriated by, the municipalities;
- (iii) the grants-in-aid to the municipalities from the Consolidated Fund of the State;

(b) the measures needed to improve the financial position of the municipalities;

(c) any other matter referred to the Finance Commission by the Governor in the interests of sound finance of the municipalities' (Constitutional Provisions, 1999: 14-15).

In response to the constitutional provisions of 1992, the states constitute their Finance Commission every five years. As per the terms of reference, SFCs recommend general principles in respect of fiscal transfers from the state government to *panchayats* and municipalities. For example, the second SFC of Uttarakhand has recommended 10 per cent of state's own revenue to be devolved to local bodies in each of the five years of the award period 2006-07 to 2010-11 (GoU, 2006). The share of rural and urban local bodies is 60 and 40 per cent respectively. The population of urban areas along with the floating and fringe population is taken into account in working out the share. Similarly, the distribution of funds among the different categories/types of urban local governments (namely municipal corporations, municipal councils and *nagar panchayats*) has been worked out on the basis of five criteria and weights assigned to each criterion—population (50%), area (15%), deprivation index (10%), remoteness index (15%) and tax effort (10%). Within this scheme of devolution, emphasis is laid on making local government authorities realise that they should make productive use of their own resources by the effective implementation of their tax laws and recovery of their dues.

Before the enactment of the 74th Amendment Act, grants were released by the state governments to local governments from specific taxes under separate heads, *viz.*, octroi compensation,[15] maintenance of roads, salary of employees, etc. The main problem with this practice was ad hoc release of grants by the state government. Urban local governments could never rely on the hope that it would receive the grants at the beginning of the financial year. The argument put forward by the state authorities is that the sources (i.e., specific taxes) from where grants were being released are not stable and this affects the flow of funds. Due to this reason, SFCs recommended the replacement of the earlier system of grants-in-aid by a more buoyant scheme of devolution (GoUP, 1996). As mentioned above, in some states a consolidated amount is transferred every year from the total net own tax receipts of the state government.

The state government authorities also prepare Action Taken Reports (ATRs) on the SFC recommendations, which indicate whether the state government had accepted a recommendation and the follow-up action it

15. Octroi has been a major source of finance for municipal governments. It is a tax on the entry of goods into a local area for consumption, use or sale therein. Many states have, however, abolished octroi with a view to remove impediments to the physical movement of goods. This has resulted in deterioration in the financial condition of urban local governments. An octroi compensatory grant was subsequently released to support urban local governments.

had taken, i.e., its implementation status. The implementation of SFC recommendations varies. In some municipalities of Uttar Pradesh, funds are received punctually every year from the state government and so the monthly salaries are paid to the functionaries on time. In the case of others (for instance in Uttarakhand), there are frequent delays in the receipt of funds, adversely affecting the governance process at the local level. Similarly in Manipur, although the second series of State Finance Commission Reports were submitted in November 2004, the state government was yet to devise a mechanism for devolution of power along with funds, as recommended by the SFC. The Twelfth Finance Commission of India highlighted a number of problems in the functioning of SFCs, and suggested corrective measures. They are as follows: (a) SFC reports should contain an estimation and analysis of the finances of state governments and local bodies at pre- and post-transfer stages along with a quantification of revenues that could be generated additionally by local bodies, as the non-availability of these data disenables the Central Finance Commission from recommending precisely the quantum of funds to be devolved to state governments for the purpose of meeting the balance resource requirements of local bodies; (b) states should avoid delays in the constitution of SFCs, their constitution in phases, frequent reconstitution, submission of reports and tabling of ATR in the legislature; (c) SFC reports should not be too dated; (d) SFCs must have as its members personages of eminence and competence; (e) SFCs must clearly identify the issues which require action on the part of the Central government; (f) state governments were found to use the grants for their own comfort and showed no sense of urgency in passing them on to the rightful recipients. This leads to withholding of further releases by the Centre and the local bodies suffer the consequences for no fault of theirs; etc. (Finance Commission, 2004: 158-159).

Municipal Bonds

In many countries of the world, public entities (such as local governments) issue government-backed bonds to raise private capital. Knowing that funds for urban services cannot be supplied through traditional means and that these can be met only with the addition of private finance, many countries have turned to municipal bond markets as the solution. Municipal bonds are standardised financial instruments that can bring buyers (i.e., investors) and sellers (i.e., bond issuers) together in the capital market. The condition is that the bond issuing authority should be creditworthy, which means there should be adequate guarantee of timely payment of interest and principal to the investors. The creditworthiness of the borrower, i.e., the municipal body, is assessed through its credit rating, which involves several factors, such as the economic base of the city, current financial position of the concerned municipal body, debt-related factors, etc.

A well-developed municipal bond system exists in the United States, which finances a large proportion of the capital investments in infrastructure. However, such bonds are rare in India because most municipalities are not creditworthy. The present municipal legislations restrict open market borrowings by municipal governments, and the state governments are reluctant to permit them to borrow. During 2000-01, the Ministry of Urban Development issued guidelines for regulating issue of tax-free municipal bonds and invited proposals from various state governments. Since then, a number of city-level agencies have been granted permission by the ministry to raise funds by issuing bonds (Table 5.1). The revenue so generated is meant to be invested for building new infrastructure as well as for augmenting the existing ones, including potable water supply, sewerage/sanitation, drainage, solid waste management, roads, bridges and flyovers, and urban transport. Under JNNURM, steps have also been taken to assess creditworthiness of municipalities. The objective is to start the process of leveraging debt for projects, and to bring ULBs in contact with banks and financial institutions.

The first institution to issue such an instrument in India without a state government guarantee was Ahmedabad Municipal Corporation (AMC). AMC identified bonds as an important source of financing its capital investment plan. Under the plan, cost estimates amounting to Rs 5,974 million (for the period 1996-97 to 2000-01) were approved for capital investments in water supply, sewerage, roads and bridges, and other services. A major part of the investment (Rs 4,890 million) was allocated for the expansion and improvement of water supply and sewerage services. With the issue of Rs 1,000 million bond by AMC, the water supply and

Table 5.1

Municipalities/Parastatal Agencies Granted Permission for Issue of Tax-free Bonds

S. No.	*Name of City-Level Agency*	*Year*	*Amount (Rs in million)*
1	Ahmedabad Municipal Corporation	2001	1000
2	Hyderabad Municipal Corporation	2002	825
3	Nashik Municipal Corporation	2003	500
4	Visakhapatnam Municipal Corporation	2003	500
5	Hyderabad Metropolitan Water Supply and Sewerage Board	2003	500
6	Ahmedabad Municipal Corporation	2004	580
7	Chennai Metropolitan Water Supply and Sewerage Board	2004	420
8	Chennai Metropolitan Water Supply and Sewerage Board	2005	500
9	Chennai Corporation	2005	448
10	Ahmedabad Municipal Corporation	2005	1000
11	Karnataka Water and Sanitation Pooled Fund Trust	2004*	1000
12	Nagpur Municipal Corporation	2007	1280
13	Ahmedabad Municipal Corporation	2007**	1500

Note: * Permission granted in 2004-05. However, revalidated during 2005-06 at the instance of the applicant.

** Revalidated during 2007-08, and further extension up to 31.3.2010 is under consideration.

Source: Ministry of Urban Development, 2010.

sewerage project was successfully financed from a number of sources, namely internal accruals of AMC (Rs 1,475 million), debt from capital markets/municipal bond (Rs 1,000 million), a loan from the USAID urban environment programme (Rs 900 million) and loans of Rs 1,515 million from other financial institutions, such as Housing and Urban Development Corporation Ltd. (HUDCO). Many scholars have noted that the issuance of the bonds was made possible mainly because of the AMC's own success in initiating reforms in financial and management practices (such as improved revenue/tax collection, adoption of new ideas and a professional work culture, development of a capital investment plan, etc.), as well as because of a congenial policy environment created by the national and the state government.

Municipal Accounting Reforms

Municipal governments' record/account[16] of their daily financial transactions are, in the main, receipt of revenues and payment of expenses[17]. In recent times, some municipalities have introduced a shift in the recording procedures from a cash-based single-entry system to an accrual-based double-entry system of accounting.

'Single-entry accounting system is a one-sided accounting entry to maintain financial information. Though most businesses maintain a record of all transactions based on the double-entry bookkeeping system, many small, simple businesses maintain only a single-entry system that records the "bare-essentials". In some cases only records of cash, accounts receivable, accounts payable and taxes paid may be maintained. Records of assets, inventory, expenses, revenues and other elements usually considered essential in an accounting system may not be kept, except in memorandum form. Single-entry systems are usually inadequate except where operations are especially simple and the volume of activity is low. This type of accounting system with additional information can typically be compiled into an income statement and balance sheet by a professional accountant. Single-entry systems are used in the interest of simplicity. They are usually less expensive to maintain than double-entry systems because they do not require the services of a trained person'.[18] Cash-based accounting is the norm in municipalities throughout India. In this form of accounting—as the name suggests—municipal revenues and expenses are recorded only if they are actually received or paid in cash, irrespective of the accounting period[19] to which they belong. It is often argued that the main problem in cash-based accounting is that it does not provide a true and fair view of the

16. 'A formal record of a particular type of transaction expressed in money or other unit of measurement and kept in a ledger' (See MoUD, 2004).

17. 'A cost relating to the operations of an accounting period or to the revenue earned during the period or the benefits of which do not extend beyond that period' (See MoUD, 2004).

18. Wikipedia, the free encyclopedia: (i) Single-entry bookkeeping system. Available from *http://en.wikipedia.org/wiki/Single-entry_bookkeeping_system*; (ii) Double-entry bookkeeping system. Available from *http://en.wikipedia.org/wiki/Double_entry_system*.

19. 'The period of time for which an operating statement is customarily prepared' (MoUD, 2004).

financial performance and position of a municipality because all credit[20] transactions are deferred to a later date, as also because single-entry records seldom make provisions for recording all transactions. In addition, many internal transactions, such as adjusting entries are often not recorded.

On the other hand, in the double-entry system,[21] transactions are recorded even though actual receipts or payments of money may not have taken place. Thus, accrual[22]-based accounting[23] results in recording of transactions and events on the basis of their substance, rather than merely when cash is received or disbursed. The main benefits of accrual-based accounting system are enumerated in Box 5.4.

Municipal accounting reforms are an outcome of the government policy for developing sustainable units of local-self government. It is envisaged that this initiative would help local bodies manage their financial matters in an efficient and effective manner, enable them to enter into PPPs, and provide them access to domestic capital markets (MoUD, 2006a). The significant steps taken by the government/ministry for the implementation of accounting reforms are listed in Box 5.5.

---

20. 'Debits and credits are a system of notation used in accounting to keep track of money movements (transactions) into and out of an account: money paid into an account is a debit; money taken out of an account is a credit. They are the most fundamental concepts in accounting, representing the two records that one party in a transaction makes on its records, transferring a money balance from one account to another, one representing a reduction of liability or increase in asset, and the other representing a balancing increase in liability or reduction of asset' (Wikipedia).
21. This system is called double-entry because each transaction is recorded in at least two accounts. Each transaction results in at least one account being debited and at least one account being credited.
22. 'Recognition of revenues and costs as they are earned or incurred (and not as money is received or paid). It includes recognition of transactions relating to assets and liabilities as they occur irrespective of the actual receipts or payments' (See MoUD, 2004).
23. 'The method of accounting whereby revenues and expenses are identified with specific periods of time, such as a month or year, and are recorded as incurred, along with acquired assets, without regard to the date of receipt or payment of cash; distinguished from cash basis' (See MoUD, 2004).

Box 5.4

Benefits of Accrual-based Double-Entry System of Accounting

- Revenue is recognised as it is earned and thus 'income'[24] constitutes both revenue received and receivable. The accrual basis not only records the actual income but also highlights the level and efficacy of revenue collection, thereby assisting decision-makers in taking financial decisions.
- Expenditure is recognised as and when the liability for payment arises and thus it constitutes both amounts paid and payable. In accrual basis of accounting, expenditure incurred on repairs and maintenance shall be recognised as expense of the period in which they are incurred and, if not paid for during the year, shall be treated as a liability (payable) and be disclosed as such in the balance sheet.
- Expenses are matched with the income earned in that year. Thus, it provides a very effective basis to understand the true performance of the organisation for the operations that is conducted in that year.
- A distinct difference is maintained between items of revenue nature and capital nature. This helps in correct presentation of financial statements,[25] i.e., the income and expenditure statement[26] and the balance sheet.[27]
- Costs which are not charged to income and expenditure account are carried forward and kept under continuous review. Any cost that appears to have lost its utility or its power to generate future revenue is written-off.

contd...

24. "Money or money equivalent earned or accrued during an accounting period, increasing the total of previously existing net assets, and arising from provision of any type of services and rentals" (See MoUD, 2004).
25. "A balance sheet, income statement (income and expenditure), receipts and payment statement or any other supporting statement or other presentation of financial data derived from accounting records" (See MoUD, 2004).
26. "A financial statement, often prepared by non-profit making entities like clubs, associations, ULBs, etc., to present their revenues and expenses for an accounting period and to show the excess of revenues over expenses (or vice-versa) for that period. It is similar to profit and loss statement and is also called revenue and expense statement" (See MoUD, 2004).
27. "A statement of the financial position of an ULB as at a given date, which exhibits its assets, liabilities, capital, reserve and other account balances at their respective book values" (See MoUD, 2004).

...contd...

- The surplus or deficit as shown at the year-end represents the correct financial position of the organisation arising out of the various transactions during that year.
- It facilitates proper financial analysis and reporting.
- It captures the 'full' cost of servicing and helps in identifying financial viability of rendering services.
- It helps in providing timely, right quality and nature of information for planning, decision-making and control at each level of management.
- It assists in effective follow-up of receivables by the municipal body and proper ascertainment of payables by the municipal body.
- One of the distinct advantages of adopting accrual accounting system is ease in financial appraisals by the financial institutions. It also facilitates credit rating through approved Credit Rating Agencies, which is a prerequisite for mobilising funds in the financial markets through debt instruments.
- It presents a true picture of the financial position of an organisation and helps in better financial management.

Source: Ministry of Urban Development, 2004.

Box 5.5

Government Initiatives towards Implementation of Municipal Accounting Reforms

- Eleventh Finance Commission devolved responsibility for exercising control and supervision over the proper maintenance of accounts and auditing of all ULBs upon Comptroller and Auditor General (C&AG) of India.
- Task Force set up by C&AG, which recommended the introduction of an accrual system of accounting, implementation of improved accounting policies and use of model budgeting and accounting formats by ULBs.
- National Seminar on Municipal Accounting Reforms organised by MoUD on January 9, 2002 to sensitise state governments for implementation of double-entry accounting system.

contd...

...contd...

- National Workshop on Municipal Accounting Reforms organised by MoUD on September 26, 2003 to review progress of state governments on municipal accounting reforms and finalise a time-bound programme for implementation of accounting reforms.
- National Municipal Accounts Manual (NMAM) prepared by A.F. Ferguson & Co. with the assistance of C&AG of India, MoUD, and USAID launched on December 31, 2004, and circulated to all states on January 11, 2005 with the objective of providing a generic framework of national municipal accounting, and supporting state governments in implementing financial management reforms at the ULB level; to enable state governments to develop state-specific municipal accounts manual.[28] NMAM details out the accounting policies, procedures, guidelines designed to ensure correct, complete and timely recording of municipal transactions and produce accurate and relevant financial reports.
- National Seminar on Municipal Accounting Reforms organised by MoUD on February 7, 2005 to sensitise stakeholders with the NMAM.
- Regional workshops held in Jaipur (August 26, 2005), Mumbai (October 21, 2005) and Bengaluru (September 22, 2006) to assess the implementation of accrual-based double-entry accounting system in the northern, western and southern regions of India.
- 'Adoption of modern accrual-based double entry system of accounting in ULBs and parastatal agencies' identified as one of the mandatory reforms for implementation at the ULB level under the JNNURM.
- National Municipal Accounting Training Manual for Elected Representatives and Top Management prepared by A.F. Ferguson & Co. with assistance of C&AG of India, MoUD, and USAID in November 2007; Manual launched on February 15, 2008; enables states to prepare state-specific training module for providing necessary training to the municipal accounts personnel in improved financial management, budgeting, accounting and auditing practices and ensure smooth transition to accrual-based system of accounting.
- Model National Municipal Assets Valuation Manual prepared and circulated to all state governments in February 2009.
- Generic municipal accounting software being developed for use by ULBs.

Source: Ministry of Urban Development, 2004; 2006a; 2007; 2010.

---

28. Andhra Pradesh Municipal Accounts Manual (APMAM) was published in 2008. Software for accrual-based accounting, namely e-Gov Financials, has also been developed. Vijayawada Municipal Corporation (VMC) has adopted the manuals and switched over to the accrual system of accounting from the financial year 2007-08. See VMC (2008).

A unique municipal finance management practice is observed in Bengaluru, where the city corporation has implemented a Fund-based Accounting System (FBAS). Recognised as a best practice by the UN Habitat, the system helps in recording financial transactions accurately under categories such as 'social', 'enterprise', 'commercial', 'fiduciary'. This approach allows the civic agency to effectively monitor its financial accounts and to administer the development works. A review of the practice reveals that: information flow cycle time has reduced considerably; civic agency's banking relationships and credibility with contractors have improved and tenders are now quoted at a much lower price.

Jawaharlal Nehru National Urban Renewal Mission (JNNURM)

The mission calls upon states/cities to undertake fiscal, financial and institutional changes for the creation of efficient and equitable urban centres. Funds for projects on urban renewal, water supply, sewerage, drainage, solid waste management, roads, flyovers, parking, urban transport, development of heritage areas, preservation of water bodies, housing, slum development, etc., are disbursed to the ULBs/parastatal agencies through designated state-level nodal agencies (SLNAs).[29] A requirement for implementation/funding of projects under JNNURM is that the projects should have the consent of the elected representatives of local bodies. The pattern of financing of infrastructure projects under the Mission is shown in Table 5.2.

Since the launch of the Mission in 2005, significant investments have been made in cities covered under JNNURM. Until September 23, 2010, a total of 527 projects costing Rs 599.18 billion under the sub-mission on urban infrastructure and governance (UIG) were approved for implementation. The Ministry of Finance has been directed to make payments to state governments without delay. Similarly, the state

---

29. Examples of SLNAs are: Andhra Pradesh Urban Finance and Infrastructure Development Corporation (APUFIDC); Haryana Urban Infrastructure Development Board (HUIDB); Karnataka Urban Infrastructure Development and Finance Corporation (KUIDFC); Maharashtra Metropolitan Regional Development Authority (MMRDA); Rajasthan Urban Infrastructure Finance and Development Corporation Ltd. (RUIFDCO); Tamil Nadu Urban Finance and Infrastructure Development Corporation (TUFIDCO); urban development/local administration/town planning departments, directorate of local bodies, development authorities, municipalities in other states.

Table 5.2

Financing Pattern of Infrastructure Projects under JNNURM

Category of Cities/Towns/UAs	*Grant*		*ULB or Parastatal Share/Loan from Financial Institutions*
	Centre	*State*	
Cities/UAs with 4 million plus population as per 2001 Census	35	15	50
Cities/UAs with million plus but less than 4 million population as per 2001 Census	50	20	30
Cities/towns/UAs in northeastern states and Jammu and Kashmir	90	10	0
Cities/UAs other than those mentioned above	80	10	10
For setting up desalination plants within 20 kms. from seashore and other urban areas predominantly facing water scarcity due to brackish water and non-availability of surface source.	80	10	10

Note: Figures shown in the table are percentages.

Source: Ministry of Urban Development, 2006b.

governments have been asked to transfer the Central funds along with their matching share to the implementing agencies immediately. The progress in the implementation of projects has, however, been fairly slow. Of the total approved 527 projects under the UIG component, only 83 (i.e., 16%) have been completed.[30] Table 5.3 shows the status of projects completed under JNNURM. The data indicate that some projects have been completed in the states of Andhra Pradesh, Delhi, Gujarat, Karnataka, Madhya Pradesh, Maharashtra, Tamil Nadu and West Bengal (Table 5.3). In the remaining states, including the northeast, Bihar, Chhattisgarh, Goa, Haryana, Himachal Pradesh, Jammu and Kashmir, Jharkhand, Orissa and Punjab, although some projects have been sanctioned, these are yet to be completed. The slow implementation of project work implies delays in further release of funds. Examples of some completed/ongoing infrastructure projects are: sewage treatment plant in Surat; filter house in Bengaluru; flyover in Hyderabad; dwelling units in Kohima, Lucknow, Bhopal, Hyderabad, Surat; water supply pump in Himmatnagar; water

30. Available from website of JNNURM: *http://jnnurm.nic.in/nurmudweb/Project/jnnurm-at-glance.pdf*

supply pumping arrangement in Mehsana; water treatment plant in Madurai; station area traffic improvement scheme in Thane; storm water drain in Pune; construction of drains in Bhiwani Mandi; restoration of facade and renewal of basic infrastructure in Connaught Place area of New Delhi; etc.

Table 5.3

Status of Projects Implemented under JNNURM

S. No.	State/UT	Projects Sanctioned (No.)	Projects Completed (No.)	Projects Completed (%)
1	Andhra Pradesh	50	15	30
2	Delhi	28	04	14
3	Gujarat	70	27	39
4	Karnataka	46	11	24
5	Madhya Pradesh	22	04	18
6	Maharashtra	79	09	11
7	Tamil Nadu	52	10	19
8	West Bengal	53	03	06

Note: So far, no project has been sanctioned in Goa, Andaman and Nicobar Islands, Dadra and Nagar Haveli, Daman and Diu and Lakshadweep.

Source: Website of JNNURM; status as on March 2011.

State governments and ULBs are also required to implement various mandatory and optional reforms before applying for funds under JNNURM. Significant financial reforms included in the mission are introduction of double-entry system of accounting, revision in property tax assessment and collection procedures, levy of reasonable user charges, effective implementation of the 74th Constitution Amendment Act provisions and rationalisation of stamp duty. Table 5.4 provides information on select mandatory reforms implemented in some Indian cities.

Pooled Finance Development Scheme

Some of the large municipalities in India have successfully mobilised resources from capital markets. For the support of other municipalities not in a position to issue bonds due to lack of capabilities, creditworthiness, and inability to prepare bankable infrastructure projects for attracting institutional financing and external funding, the Central government launched a pooled finance development scheme (PFDS) in 2006. Under the

Table 5.4

Financial Reforms Accomplished under JNNURM

S. No.	Financial Reforms	Cities which have Accomplished Reforms
1	Shift to double-entry accounting	Hyderabad, Vijayawada, Visakhapatnam, Raipur, Ahmedabad, Rajkot, Surat, Vadodara, Shimla, Kochi, Thiruvananthapuram, Bengaluru, Mysore, Bhopal, Indore, Ujjain, Nagpur, Nashik, Pune, Greater Mumbai, Ludhiana, Bhubaneswar, Puri, Jaipur, Ajmer, Coimbatore, Madurai, Chennai, Agartala, Agra, Allahabad, Kanpur, Lucknow, Meerut, Varanasi, Asansol, Kolkata
2	Property tax: 85% coverage	Hyderabad, Vijayawada, Visakhapatnam, Raipur, Ahmedabad, Rajkot, Surat, Vadodara, Thiruvananthapuram, Bengaluru, Mysore, Pune, Greater Mumbai, Puducherry, Coimbatore, Madurai, Chennai, Agra, Allahabad, Asansol, Kolkata
3	Property tax: 90% collection efficiency	Hyderabad, Vijayawada, Visakhapatnam, Chandigarh, Ahmedabad, Rajkot, Vadodara, Mysore, Pune, Coimbatore, Madurai, Chennai, Allahabad, Lucknow, Asansol
4	Operation and maintenance for water supply: 100% cost recovery	Visakhapatnam, Nashik, Pune, Greater Mumbai, Coimbatore, Chennai, Madurai
5	Solid waste management: 100% cost recovery	Hyderabad, Visakhapatnam, Nashik, Pune, Greater Mumbai, Chennai

Source: Overall status of implementation of reforms, 2011.[31]

scheme, a pooled finance development fund (PFDF) has been set up for municipalities to provide them credit enhancement grants to access market borrowings through pooled financing bonds for investment in urban infrastructure projects. Each state/Union Territory is expected to designate either an existing state pooled finance entity (SPFE), or create a new entity for the execution of PFDS. As per the guidelines, SPFEs would: (i) work with and support ULBs in urban infrastructure project development; (ii) select projects for financing from the ones suggested by ULBs based on viability and priority; (iii) get the projects appraised by recognised credit rating agency, which will determine credit rating enhancement fund (CREF) requirement for investment grade rating of the project; (iv) mobilise resources from local capital and financial markets by issue of bonds to fund

31. Available from *http://jnnurm.nic.in/nurmudweb/Reforms/overall_status.pdf*

viable/bankable local infrastructure projects; (v) provide sub-loans to ULBs, or purchase bonds of ULBs; (vi) provide for escrowing of resources for repayment of loan; (vii) sign agreement with the Central government; (viii) sign appropriate grant and loan agreements with the ULB; (ix) make application through the state/Union Territory government for reimbursement of Central grant for project development and contribution to CREF; (x) set up and manage CREF and (xi) prepare projects that meet acceptable technical, environmental and financial requirements.[32]

SPFEs would be supported by the Central government through PFDF. Of the funds made available, 5 per cent would be utilised for project development assistance. The balance of 95 per cent would be utilised for contribution to CREF to improve the credit rating of municipal bonds to investment grade. This fund would serve as the third tier of security in case the first two tiers, *viz.*, escrowing of resources of ULB and any other internal arrangement between a state and the SPFE including state intercept, for some reason, fail to meet repayment obligations. Three-fourths (75 per cent) of the cost of the project development for each municipality would be reimbursed by the Centre and 25 per cent by the state/UT/ULB. A provision of Rs 25 billion has already been earmarked in the Eleventh Five Year Plan (2007-2012) for the scheme. The progress and achievements under the scheme are listed in Box 5.6.

Property Tax Reforms

Property tax is levied by local governments on owners/occupiers of buildings and land situated within municipal limits. It is mandatory for the citizens, who are users of various civic services, to pay this tax to the municipality. As municipal budgets show, the income from property tax is substantial, but, as noted earlier, it is seldom collected in full. Numerous efforts have been made to reform property tax assessment and collection procedures. In this sub-section, the main concepts, issues and initiatives concerning property tax are described.

Civic agencies in India generally calculate the amount of property tax to be paid by residents on the basis of the annual rental value (ARV) of the

32. Guidelines for Pooled Finance Development Scheme (PFDS), Available from website of Ministry of Urban Development.

Box 5.6

Pooled Finance Development Scheme: Progress and Achievements

- PFDS approved by the Central government on September 29, 2006.
- Resolution conveying decision of the government issued on October 25, 2006.
- All state/UT governments requested (during October and December 2006) to take necessary preparatory action for operationalisation of the scheme in accordance with the scheme guidelines to avail benefit.
- Scheme formally launched in a National Workshop organised in Chennai on November 20, 2006 to sensitise state governments and all stakeholders for implementation of the scheme in a time-bound manner. Regional workshop held in Kolkata on February 21, 2007 and in Shillong on April 5, 2007.
- Tentative allocation of Rs 4 billion made for the scheme under Tenth Five Year Plan (2002-2007). During 2006-07, Rs 500 million provided for the scheme. Rs 1 billion provided to MoUD for 2007-08 for PFDF and provision of Rs 25 billion made for Eleventh Plan Period (2007-2012).
- Matter pursued at the Chief Secretary and Chief Minister level during January and March 2007 to expedite setting up of SPFEs in states/UTs.
- Necessary amendment made to the Income Tax Act on May 11, 2007 to provide exemption in respect of interest on bonds issued by a SPFE and specified by Central government by notification in the official gazette; guidelines for issue of tax-free pooled finance development bonds issued on June 7, 2007.
- States of Andhra Pradesh, Assam, Karnataka, Kerala, Nagaland, Orissa, Rajasthan and Tamil Nadu have set up their SPFE for implementation of scheme; first proposal for issue of tax-free pooled finance development bond worth Rs 450 million was received from water and sanitation pooled fund, the designated SPFE of Tamil Nadu; proposal notified by Department of Revenue in the official gazette on January 14, 2008.

Source: Ministry of Urban Development (2006a: 33-35; 2010: 32-33) and Eleventh Five Year Plan of Planning Commission.

property (i.e., land and building). Most enactments/municipal laws define ARV as the 'gross annual rent at which a property may reasonably be expected to let from year to year'. In this definition, the property tax base apparently consists of the rent which a property could be reasonably expected to fetch in the market. Application of such an abstract concept in a real situation has been one of the major problems confronting property tax assessees. Using standard rent as the criteria for evaluating municipal properties is becoming obsolete in the fast changing real estate market in the country.

The deficiencies in the definition of ARV result in unrealistic estimation of annual rental value by the municipal staff. It allows the functionaries to indulge in ad hoc and discretionary practices in the calculation of ARV. Since calculation of ARV is a discretionary practice, value of all other taxes (namely water, sewer, conservancy, etc.) linked to property tax is also affected. For example, if ARV is undervalued or over-valued, service tax collection is affected adversely. Often, service tax receipts are much below the service operation and maintenance expenditure incurred by urban local governments. Furthermore, the property tax system suffers from other problems. For instance, in several large cities, there is a constant addition to the number of properties. However, their enumeration is not undertaken by the local government regularly due to various reasons. This leads to a large number of properties being left out of the tax net. The problem of under enumeration is also because many citizens do not register their properties so as to evade tax payment. Added to this is the fact that periodic assessment of property tax rates is not carried out, so that the old rates continued for several years. Given these problems, it is estimated that the actual amount of property tax collected annually stay below 50 to 60 per cent of the total tax demand (i.e., the amount that should have been collected) in most of the country's municipalities.

With increasing realisation that property tax has considerable potential to augment local revenues, urban governments in some Indian states have initiated reforms in the system. The effort has been to adopt valuation procedures that are simple, transparent and acceptable to the people. Some of these measures are:

- modification in the definition of ARV as 'the rent that a property is capable of fetching over a period of one year';
- adoption of an 'area-based' assessment method for calculating the rent fetching capability of a property—classification of properties based on their—location (i.e., principal main road, main road, etc.), use (i.e., purely residential, purely commercial/industrial, etc.) and type of construction (i.e., *pucca* building with reinforced cement concrete (RCC) roof, *pucca* building with asbestos/corrugated sheet roof, etc.) and calculating ARV of property with reference to its location, type of construction, plinth area, age of building, and the nature of use to which it is put;
- removing the use of ARV as a tax base by linking it directly to key property characteristics, leaving the actual tax level to be decided by the local authorities within a range specified by the state government;
- delinking of service taxes from ARV;
- mandatory periodic revision of tax rates;
- dispensing with the demand notice for the tax and putting the responsibility on property owners for timely tax payment;
- relief to buildings constructed under the weaker section housing scheme and to owner-occupied residential buildings;
- concessions to elderly, women, handicapped persons and ex-servicemen;
- online filing of returns and payment of property tax;
- use of GIS mapping and self-assessment practices to enhance efficiency and transparency in property tax assessment.

A review of literature on the performance of urban local governments following the introduction of property tax reforms reveals significant increases in income, as well as considerable reduction in taxation disputes due to adoption of simple and non-discretionary practices (MCD, 2005: 36). In Bengaluru, for example, the civic agency implemented a Self Assessment Scheme (SAS) to allow owners of properties to submit the declaration of assessment of property tax based on unit area value. This initiative was undertaken to introduce objectivity, transparency and simplicity in property tax assessment. To guide the citizens in self-assessing their properties and timely payment, a property tax handbook has been designed for their convenience, which is available on the municipal website. Such measures have not only helped the civic agency in raising revenues, but have also instilled confidence in the tax payer.

Case Study of Financial Reforms in Kolkata

Kolkata is selected as a case study because the corporation has experienced a high growth in its income during the last three years, which makes it a textbook case for studying the factors that have contributed to this growth.

Kolkata is the capital of the state of West Bengal. The population of Kolkata (municipal corporation including Joka outgrowth) at the time of 2001 Census was 4.58 million, and its geographical area was 187.33 sq km. The city also receives a daily floating population of about six million. Kolkata acquired the civic status of a municipal corporation in 1876 and is governed by the provisions of the Kolkata Municipal Corporation (KMC) Act, 1980 (Datta and Alam, 2008).

For administrative purposes, the KMC area is divided into 141 municipal wards that are grouped into 15 boroughs.

Duties of the Corporation

KMC is responsible for general administration and provision of a range of services to the city residents, including the supply of drinking water, sewerage and drainage, solid waste management, roads maintenance, street lighting, slum development works, parks and gardens, land use control and building, health care, town planning and architecture, primary education, etc. The activities undertaken by the municipal functionaries in respect of various services are shown in Table 5.5.

Table 5.5

Activities undertaken by KMC

S. No.	*KMC Services*	*Activities*
1	Assessment	Identification of premises; determination of annual value of property; mutation of property, collection of property tax
2	Amusement	Issue of licence for theatres, circus, fairs, exhibitions, cyber cafes, cable TV operators, lottery operators, restaurants, hotels, clubs, etc.
3	Advertisement	Issue of licence for outdoor advertisements, control of nuisance created by unauthorised advertisement, construction and maintenance of bus passenger shelters
4	Births and deaths	Registration of births and deaths, and issue of certificates
5	Building sanction	Extending sanction for erection of new building, renovation of existing building; stopping/demolishing unauthorised construction; regularising construction of unauthorised building on receipt of penalty
6	Slum development	Physical improvement/augmentation, monitoring and maintenance of municipal services
7	Centre/state schemes	Implementation and coordination of schemes/programmes– old age pension, maternity/family benefit; implementation of entrepreneurship development by providing loans/grants to the entrepreneurs
8	Car parking	Providing safe car parking facilities to citizens
9	Records	Preserving registers and documents pertaining to birth, death, building plans, assessment, trade licences, survey plans, etc.
10	Sewerage and drainage	Drainage of waste water; operation/maintenance of drainage pumping stations; cleaning/maintenance of underground sewers, open and covered drains; removal of water logging and cleaning choked sewers; according sanction of premises; house drainage plan and its connection to city sewerage
11	Education	Extending primary education; organising educational programmes
12	Street lighting	Installation/maintenance of lights in streets, gardens and parks, electric crematoriums, schools, etc.
13	Solid waste	Collection/transportation of waste, maintenance of landfill sites, street sweeping and washing
14	Trade licence	Issuance and renewal of trade licence
15	Water supply	Generation and distribution of water

Source: *https://www.kmcgov.in/KMCPortal/jsp/KMCPortalHome1.jsp*

Receipt and Expenditure Pattern

KMC obtains funds to execute its duties from various internal and external sources. Internal sources include receipts from taxes, non-taxes and PPPs. External sources comprise receipts from Centre, state, other grants and loans. Revised estimate of KMC receipts for the year 2007-08 is Rs 20.51 billion.[33] The share of both internal and external sources in the total KMC receipts for 2007-08 is about 50 per cent each (Table 5.6). A comparison with the 2006-07 actual receipts (pre-audited) shows an increase in KMC receipts by more than Rs 5 billion (Annexure Table A-5.1).

Table 5.6

Receipts of Kolkata Municipal Corporation, 2007-08

S. No.	*Particulars*	*Revised Estimate (Rs in Million)*	*Per cent to Total Receipts of KMC*
A	Internal sources		
1	Tax revenue (such as property, trade, advertisement, carriages and carts, etc.)	3,520.51	17.16
2	Non-tax revenue (such as receipts from water supply, sewerage and drainage, municipal markets, building plan sanction and licence fees, etc.)	3,869.54	18.86
3	Receipt from public-private partnerships	3,068.20	14.96
	Total receipts from internal sources (A 1+2+3)	10,458.25	50.98
B	External sources (Centre/state/other grants and loans)		
1	State government grant (such as grants for dearness allowance and increased cost of pay, special grant for CESC, entertainment, relief on pension, etc.)	4,513.35	22.00
2	Suspense heads—contra (such as NSDP, KEIP, JNNURM, DFID, MPLAD scheme, Twelfth Finance Commission, SFC, deposits and advances to corporation employees and contractors, etc.)	5,544.12	27.02
	Total receipts from external sources (B 1+2)	10,057.47	49.02
	Total receipts (A+B)	20,515.72	100.00

Source: Kolkata Municipal Corporation (2008a).

33. The total receipts of the corporation for the year 2010-11 are estimated at Rs 21.9 billion (Kolkata Municipal Corporation, Interim Revised Budget Statement for 2010-11).

Among internal sources, revenue receipts during 2007-08 from property tax, PPPs, and building plan sanction fee were substantial. Other important sources were receipts from sewerage and drainage, water supply, licence fees, municipal markets and advertisements. KMC also obtains funds from the Centre, state and other agencies in the form of grants and loans. Significant among these are: grant for increased cost of pay and dearness allowance, special grant for Calcutta Electricity Supply Corporation (CESC), NSDP,[34] KEIP,[35] JNNURM, Department for International Development, UK (DFID), Member of Parliament Local Area Development (MPLAD) scheme, Twelfth Finance Commission, State Finance Commission, etc. Estimates of receipts for the year 2008-09 show that grant under JNNURM will increase to Rs 2.51 billion from Rs 448.2 million during 2007-08 (Annexure Table A-5.1).

Revised estimates of KMC expenditure for the year 2007-08 are shown in Annexure Table A-5.2. The total expenditure incurred by the corporation during this period was Rs 20.85 billion.[36] Major items of expenditure include water supply, sewerage and drainage, roads, footpaths, parks and squares, solid waste management, administration and support, electricity charges and creation of assets under PPPs. Against the grants and loans received from the Centre, state government and other agencies, high expenses were incurred under schemes such as NSDP, KEIP, JNNURM, DFID, MPLAD, etc.

Impact of Financial Reforms Initiated by the Corporation

KMC functionaries have identified three areas to which attention is being given, i.e., strengthening basic infrastructure—roads, pipes, drains, tunnels, health, education, etc.; qualitative improvement in e-infrastructure and business process re-engineering. To attend to these, as

34. National Slum Development Programme (NSDP) is a centrally assisted scheme introduced in 1996 for improving the living condition in slums by providing basic services to the poor people.

35. Kolkata Environmental Improvement Project (KEIP) is a scheme initiated by the KMC for addressing problems of environmental degradation and improving quality of life in Kolkata.

36. The total expenditure of the corporation for the year 2010-11 is estimated at Rs 24.48 billion (Kolkata Municipal Corporation, Interim Revised Budget Statement for 2010-11).

well as other duties in an efficient and responsible manner, the corporation has undertaken a number of steps to strengthen its financial position (KMC, 2008b). The initiatives are described below.

Accounting Reforms and Audit of Accounts

KMC is in the process of shifting to the accrual-based double-entry system of accounting, and efforts are on to make the entire accounting system computerised. The new practice is already in use in select KMC departments. The earlier cash-based system is being discontinued due to several disadvantages, one of the major flaws being that the code does not indicate the cost centre and location of income/expenditure. Furthermore, KMC has ensured that its accounts are audited regularly through internal audit as against external audit to protect their exchequer. Prior to 2003-04, audit of accounts was undertaken after long periods of time. Other ongoing reforms are financial process re-engineering, computerised pay-roll system, and restructuring of budget system. Credit Rating and Information Services of India Ltd. (CRISIL), an independent credit rating agency engaged by the MoUD for corporate credit rating of various municipal corporations, has observed substantial progress in KMC finances and accordingly rated the corporation as 'A+ stable'. A high rating implies greater possibilities of obtaining loans from various agencies.

Property Tax Reforms

The government of West Bengal has recently initiated the process of improving the existing system used in municipal property taxation for raising recovery from this source. The new method is viewed as an equitable and transparent system of valuation of properties. In the earlier system, based on the principle of annual rateable value, a number of problems were experienced: difficulties in calculating reasonable rent for various types of properties; tendency to mis-report the rent; poor compliance by citizens; frequent litigation by the assessees and no scope for self-assessment. The Kolkata Municipal Corporation (Amendment) Act, 2006 and the Kolkata Municipal Corporation (Municipal Valuation Committee) Rule, 2007 provide for a unit area method of valuation of properties. As per the new method, the entire city is divided into 262 blocks and further classified into seven categories (A to G) on the basis of land value, infrastructure and facilities available. A base unit area value is assigned to each category after publishing a draft notification in official gazette to obtain suggestions and objections from citizens within 60 days. For this purpose, a Municipal Valuation Committee and an Anomaly Review Committee comprising experts from different fields are formed to consider citizen's feedback in the categorisation of blocks. Multiplicative factors (capturing variations in property size, purpose of use, age and location of property, nature of occupancy and type of structure) are reviewed to account for the wide heterogeneity among properties within a block. Furthermore, the covered space of building (or area of land) and a flat tax rate (independent of the annual valuation of the property) within a limit of 6 to 20 per cent are the other indicators used in the calculation of the annual tax payable. The assessment of the property is done by the assessees themselves by using the following formula:

Annual tax payable (Rs/annum) =
Category-wise base unit area value (Rs/sq ft/annum) ×
Multiplicative factors ×
Covered space of building/area of land (sq ft) ×
Tax rate (%)

PPPs and Monetisation of Land

KMC has taken steps to monetise the idly lying vacant land for generating revenue. This is being done by giving vacant land to interested private agencies on lease for its development. A one time royalty is paid by the private agencies to KMC, which is valid until the lease expires. The private sector has also been involved in the development of infrastructure and markets. The eastern metropolitan by-pass road, which connects Salt Lake and Dum Dum localities to central Kolkata, is an example of a project completed by adopting a PPP approach.

Such initiatives have helped the corporation in generating revenue of Rs 3.07 billion during 2007-08, which accounts for nearly 15 per cent of the total receipts of KMC (Table 5.6). The funds so generated by KMC are being used to repay debt. The corporation is also in a position to undertake various infrastructure projects sanctioned under JNNURM, since the JNNURM funding pattern requires large municipalities to mobilise 50 per cent of the total sanctioned amount (Table 5.2).

Conclusion

This chapter has described significant financial problems experienced by municipalities and the government policy initiatives aimed at strengthening municipal finance. The important lessons learnt from an assessment of recent developments on the subject are summarised below.

An aggregate grant of Rs 231.11 billion has been recommended by the Thirteenth Finance Commission of India for municipalities in all states for the period 2010-15. The funds are released through state governments to enable municipalities to discharge their primary functions. This amount is a substantial increase over the grants recommended by the previous commissions[37] and is in addition to the normal flow of funds to the local bodies from the states and the amounts that flow from the implementation of SFC recommendations.

A finance commission is constituted in each state of India every five years to review the financial position of municipalities and make recommendations on the measures needed to improve their financial position. The implementation of SFC recommendations varies across municipalities. At some places, funds are received every year from the state government. At others, there are frequent delays in the transfer of funds, which affects adversely the efficient functioning of municipalities.

Some civic agencies functioning in the states of Andhra Pradesh, Gujarat, Karnataka, Maharashtra and Tamil Nadu have successfully generated funds by issuing tax-free municipal bonds. The revenue generated in this manner provides for the creation of new infrastructure as well as augmentation of existing systems.

For municipalities which are not in a position to issue bonds due to lack of capabilities, creditworthiness, and inability to prepare bankable infrastructure projects, the Indian government has launched a pooled finance development scheme to enable local bodies to fund their urban infrastructure projects. A provision of Rs 25 billion has already been made for the scheme during the Eleventh Five Year Plan period (2007-2012). The

37. The Eleventh Finance Commission recommended a grant of Rs 4 billion for municipalities for each of the five years beginning 2000-01, which was increased to Rs 50 billion for 2005-2010.

states of Andhra Pradesh, Assam, Karnataka, Kerala, Nagaland, Orissa, Rajasthan and Tamil Nadu have set up the necessary mechanism for implementation of the scheme.

Some municipalities have modified the procedures involved in recording their financial transactions, i.e., there is a shift from a cash-based single-entry system to an accrual-based double-entry system of accounting. In the double-entry system, transactions are recorded even though actual receipts or payments of money may not have taken place, which helps in providing timely, right quality and nature of information required for planning, decision-making and control at each level of management.

The Centre has kept a substantial provision of funds under JNNURM as reform-linked Central assistance for funding infrastructure projects on urban renewal, water supply, sanitation, drainage, road network, urban transport, housing, slum development, etc. A number of states have initiated the process of project and reform implementation, and shown progress in completion of works. However, the slow pace of implementation is a matter of concern since this leads to delays in further release of funds.

Local governments in some Indian states have initiated reforms in property tax assessment and collection procedures to improve recovery from this source, such as: modifications in the definition of ARV for a realistic assessment; regular enumeration of properties; delinking of service taxes from ARV; mandatory periodic revision of tax rates; etc. With the introduction of simple, transparent and non-discretionary practices, a number of municipalities have experienced an increase in municipal revenues, as well as a considerable reduction in taxation disputes.

Similarly, an assessment of the financial data and information pertaining to Kolkata Municipal Corporation, the case study for this research, shows a positive impact of the measures undertaken by the civic agency. The financial condition of KMC has improved over time. Recent data (KMC, 2008b: 6) show that internal mobilisation, which was 50 per cent of the total budget till a few years ago, has risen to 68 per cent.

KMC has also recorded an increase in revenue from licence fee, amusement fee, advertisement tax, parking fee, building plan sanction fee, etc. This upward trend is an indication of the financial strength of the corporation. It is observed that this growth is not only due to additional grants received but also because of an emphasis on internal mobilisation of resources. In this context, it is noted that with the introduction of accounting reforms and an emphasis on internal audit of accounts, the corporation has acquired an 'A+ stable' ranking by a reputed national credit rating agency, namely CRISIL. This implies greater possibilities of obtaining loans from various agencies. Next, necessary steps have been taken to switch over to the unit area system of valuation of properties for a more realistic assessment of property values. It is expected that recovery from this source would increase by many times with the adoption of the new system. Interested parties have been asked to inform the municipal body as to whether they favoured the proposal for establishing an integrated enterprise-level geographical information system to aid the KMC in strategic planning, resource mobilisation and utilisation, managing operations, and streamlining municipal taxation. Finally, PPPs in land, markets and infrastructure development by monetisation of vacant land are other important activities vigorously pursued by the corporation. This initiative has helped the corporation in generating revenue of Rs 3.07 billion during 2007-08, which accounts for nearly 15 per cent of the total receipts of the KMC. It is to be noted that this amount has shown an increase by nearly two times over the previous year (2006-07), when it was Rs 1.56 billion. The funds so generated by the KMC are used to repay debt, and the civic agency is also in a position to undertake various infrastructure projects sanctioned under the JNNURM. Furthermore, it is learnt that the KMC has not proposed any changes in the fee/tax rates, such as licence fee, amusement fee, advertisement tax, parking fee and building plan sanction fee.

In conclusion it may be stated that mobilisation and management of funds at local government level continues to be a tough task. Accordingly, this study puts forward the following suggestions:

- Transfer of funds from the Central and state government to local governments should take place without any delays; procedural bottlenecks should be identified and appropriately addressed.

- Fund requirements should be correctly estimated by the local bodies after giving due consideration to their functional domain and population projections, and by involving citizen's representatives.
- Greater transparency should be promoted in municipal finance practices; views of all municipal functionaries and citizens should be considered before spending funds on any development work.
- Expertise should be developed among municipal functionaries through capacity building programmes for optimal utilisation of funds received from the Centre and state government; programmes should give adequate importance to mobilisation of funds, financial management, levying new taxes, transfer of funds generated on account of shared taxes, raising loans, budget formulation, enforcement of bye-laws, regular auditing of accounts, private sector participation in land and infrastructure development, regular enumeration of properties, etc.
- Costs incurred by local governments in the provision of civic services, such as water supply, sewerage, waste collection and disposal, etc., should be estimated accurately, and differential tax rates and service charges should be appropriately finalised in consultation with technical experts as well as citizen's representatives belonging to various income strata; municipal functionaries should be accordingly trained for this purpose; impact of efficient financial management on infrastructure and service delivery should be demonstrated to citizens for improved cost recovery.
- Municipal functionaries should be guided in the award of service contracts to local private operators for the operation and maintenance of various civic services. Such innovative practices will help in meeting the growing shortage of funds, equipment and manpower.

References

Constitutional Provisions Relating to Village *Panchayats* and Municipalities in India. (1999). Lucknow: Eastern Book Company.

Datta, L.N. and Afroze Alam (2008). *Kolkata Municipal Corporation Act, 1980*. Kolkata: Tax 'N Law Publishers.

Finance Commission (2004). *Report of the Twelfth Finance Commission (2005-2010)*. New Delhi: Government of India.

Government of India (1966). *Report of the Rural-Urban Relationship Committee* Vol. I. New Delhi: Ministry of Health and Family Planning.

———. (1963). "Augmentation of Financial Resources of Urban Local Bodies", Report of the Committee of Ministers Constituted by the Central Council of Local Self-Government. New Delhi: Government of India.

Government of Uttarakhand (2006). *Second State Finance Commission Report*. Dehradun. Available from *http://gov.ua.nic.in/sfc/*

Government of Uttar Pradesh (1996). *Final Report of the State Finance Commission* Vol. 1. Lucknow.

Kolkata Municipal Corporation (2008a). Mayor's Budget Estimates of Receipts and Expenditures on the Revenue Fund and Suspense Heads (Contra) for the Year 2008-09", Vol. II, *Detailed Heads of Accounts and Allocation of Funds*.

———. (2008b). "Budget Statement by Mayor, Kolkata for 2008-2009". Kolkata: Central Municipal Office.

Ministry of Finance (2007). *The Gazette of India: Extraordinary*, Part II – Section 3 (ii). Department of Economic Affairs Notification,13 November 2007.

Ministry of Urban Development (2010). *Annual Report 2009-10*. New Delhi: Government of India.

———. (2009). *Newsletter* 1(1), January.

———. (2007). *National Municipal Accounting Training Manual for Elected Representatives and Top Management*.

———. (2006a). *Annual Report 2006-07*. New Delhi: Government of India. p.42.

———. (2006b). *Modified Guidelines for Projects of JNNURM*.

———. (2004). "Definitions, Accounting Concepts and Accounting Conventions", Chapter 2: *National Municipal Accounts Manual*.

Municipal Corporation of Delhi (2005). *Civic Guide*. Delhi: Press and Information Office. p.36.

Planning Commission. *Eleventh Five Year Plan 2007-2012*, Vol. III. New Delhi: Government of India.

Sachdeva, Pardeep (1993). *Urban Local Government and Administration in India*. Allahabad: Kitab Mahal.

Vijayawada Municipal Corporation. (2008). *Financial Statements for the Year 2007-08*.

Annexure Table A-5.1

Receipts of Kolkata Municipal Corporation

(Rs in lakh)

S. No.	Particulars	Estimate 2008-09	Revised Estimate 2007-08	Actual Pre-Audited 2006-07
I	Revenue receipt (internal source)			
(a)	Tax revenue			
1.	Property tax including surcharge on property tax	38,140.00	33,400.00	27,608.44
2.	Tax on trades, professions & callings	39.00	33.50	31.15
3.	Tax on advertisement	1,645.00	1,145.00	471.95
4.	Service charges on Central govt. properties	575.00	575.00	484.87
5.	Tax on carriages	0.91	0.81	0.53
6.	Tax on carts	60.80	50.80	33.80
	Total tax revenue	40,460.71	35,205.11	28,630.74
(b)	Non-tax revenue			
1.	Receipt from water supply	3,895.50	3,530.50	2,930.49
2.	Receipt from sale of water to ships (for drinking, washing purposes)	255.00	300.00	157.43
3.	Receipt from sewerage & drainage	4,448.00	4,028.20	3,076.81
4.	Receipt from commercial services (municipal markets, etc.)	1,301.46	1,302.77	1,326.98
5.	Receipt from land & estates	316.60	199.60	180.41
6.	Receipt from building plan sanction fees	16,168.60	14,589.90	14,937.45
7.	Receipt from licence fees	2,902.00	2,898.50	1,991.99
8.	Receipt from solid waste management (KMC levies conservancy charge)	182.99	182.14	138.31
9.	Receipt from health services	593.04	562.69	473.64
10.	Receipt from amusement fees	228.10	200.60	173.55
11.	Receipt from car parking fees	1,200.00	650.00	459.76
12.	Receipt from sale of condemned materials (such as nuts, bolts, etc., lying in KMC store are sold through bidding)	100.00	100.00	5.61
13.	Unclassified receipts (for example, marriage hall is given to citizens and a fee is charged by KMC)	10,703.70	10,150.55	6,963.95
	Total non-tax revenue	42,294.99	38,695.45	32,816.38
(c)	Receipt from public-private partnership	24,010.00	30,682.00	15,605.90
	Total revenue from internal source (a+b+c)	106,765.70	104,582.56	77,053.02

contd...

...contd...

S. No.	*Particulars*	*Estimate 2008-09*	*Revised estimate 2007-08*	*Actual pre-Audited 2006-07*
II	Government grant (state)			
1.	Grant for dearness allowance	8,200.00	7,100.00	8,255.75
2.	Grant for increased cost of pay	25,000.00	23,000.00	19,134.15
3.	Grant out of the proceeds of motor vehicle tax	337.50	337.50	—
4.	Other grants	500.00	630.00	684.57
5.	Special grant for Calcutta Electricity Supply Corporation (CESC)	11,520.00	10,560.00	12,432.00
6.	Grant out of the proceeds of entertainment	1,200.00	1,200.00	1,105.55
7.	Relief on pension	3,000.00	2,306.00	1,105.14
	Total government grant	49,757.50	45,133.50	42,717.16
	Total revenue receipt	156,523.20	149,716.06	119,770.18
III.	Suspense heads (contra)			
	Centre/state/other grants and loans			
1.	Basic minimum service	—	—	—
2.	National Slum Development Programme (NSDP)	1,000.00	1,000.00	—
3.	National Social Assistance Programme (NSAP)	500.00	400.00	107.05
4.	Kolkata Environmental Improvement Project (KEIP)	24,025.00	17,945.00	1,137.95
5.	Jawaharlal Nehru National Urban Renewal Mission (JNNURM)	25,172.00	4,482.00	1,234.37
6.	Department for International Development (DFID)	6,830.00	4,940.20	1,099.55
7.	MP Local Area Development Scheme (MPLAD)	4,000.00	3,200.00	3,882.37
8.	Bidhayak Elaka Unnayan Prakalpa (BEUP)	225.00	200.00	286.66
9.	Wage Employment Scheme	220.00	220.00	—
10.	Schemes under Ganga Action Plan	200.00	—	450.00
11.	Water Supply Programme for Mega City Plan	—	—	—
12.	Programme for installation of water meters	100.00	—	—
13.	Calcutta Urban Development Programme–III (Health)	80.00	80.00	72.56
14.	VAMBAY works (providing small quarters)	150.00	100.00	68.50
15.	Corpus fund (donations by NRIs for maintenance of historical monuments)	675.00	100.00	433.00
16.	Eleventh Finance Commission	—	—	—
17.	Twelfth Finance Commission	1,896.00	1,265.00	1,268.71
18.	State Finance Commission	1,698.00	1,133.00	566.25

contd...

...contd...

S. No.	*Particulars*	*Estimate 2008-09*	*Revised estimate 2007-08*	*Actual pre-Audited 2006-07*
19.	Non-convertible revenue bond	—	—	—
20.	Miscellaneous agencies	8,401.00	8,351.00	5,476.26
21.	Cost of work done in default	—	—	—
22.	Stores purchase	—	25.00	67.78
23.	Redevelopment of municipal market	100.00	600.00	560.41
24.	Deposit & advances to corporation employees	5,714.00	5,715.00	5,463.94
25.	Deposit & advances to contractors	6,210.00	5,685.00	10,808.92
26.	Short/medium-term loan	—	—	—
	Total contra heads (receipt)	87,196.00	55,441.20	32,984.28
	Total revenue receipt	156,523.20	149,716.06	119,770.18
	Total receipt (revenue + suspense)	243,719.20	205,157.26	152,754.46

Source: Kolkata Municipal Corporation (2008a). Mayor's budget estimates for 2008-09.

Annexure Table A-5.2

Expenditure of Kolkata Municipal Corporation

(Rs in lakh)

S. No.	*Particulars*	*Estimate 2008-09*	*Revised Estimate 2007-08*	*Actual Pre-Audited 2006-07*
	Revenue Expenditure			
1.	Water supply	22,768.20	20,793.55	11,798.52
2.	Water supply to ships	206.79	188.63	100.87
3.	Sewerage & drainage	15,087.38	14,115.03	6,882.29
4.	Roads, footpaths, parks & squares	21,883.14	18,127.41	12,208.36
5.	Lighting	5,420.76	4,646.32	3,152.77
6.	Electricity	442.40	427.45	277.52
7.	Solid waste management (SWM) – I	22,401.09	20,559.32	14,250.54
8.	Motor vehicles (SWM-II)	2,353.19	2,077.20	1,736.27
9.	Commercial services (municipal markets)	1,170.25	1,028.86	676.13
10.	Education services	1,638.91	1,479.81	1,159.32
11.	Health services	7,259.11	5,869.28	3,465.08
12.	*Bustee*/slum service	8,641.51	5,475.58	3,033.98
13.	Administration & support	19,213.32	15,839.68	10,250.41
14.	Loan charges	150.00	204.21	575.17
15.	Electricity charges	13,800.00	13,200.00	15,146.93
16.	Security arrangement	550.00	500.00	440.28

contd...

...*contd*...

S. No.	*Particulars*	*Estimate 2008-09*	*Revised Estimate 2007-08*	*Actual Pre-Audited 2006-07*
	Special programmes			
1.	Councillors' Elaka Unnayan Prakalpa	705.00	713.34	605.54
2.	Integrated Borough scheme	1,680.00	2,563.76	950.66
3.	Funds at the disposal of mayor	700.00	650.00	31.28
4.	Funds at the disposal of municipal commissioner	200.00	130.00	105.24
5.	Contribution of pension fund	9,300.00	8,900.00	11,525.60
6.	Contribution from revenue for JNNURM	7,000.00	767.00	—
7.	Restructuring of municipal government	10.00	10.00	8.90
8.	Funds under chief engineer (civil)	40.00	100.00	67.47
9.	Funds under chief engineer (planning and development)	40.00	40.00	25.26
10.	Contribution of revenue for KEIP	2,725.00	—	—
11.	Waiver of house building loan	20.00	20.00	9.20
12.	Group insurance	35.00	35.00	—
13.	Leave travel concession	70.00	70.00	2.86
14.	Promotion of cultural activities	30.00	30.00	0.10
15.	Parks & playgrounds	—	75.00	6.66
16.	Special development works	600.00	600.00	15.06
17.	Grant to charitable & educational institutions, etc.	100.00	100.00	54.00
18.	Renovation/improvement of historical & other buildings of KMC	920.00	480.00	105.71
19.	Promotion of sports & coaching	—	30.00	1.39
20.	Cost for special & advisory committee for implementation of KMC Act & rule	5.00	5.00	0.36
21.	Programmes on environment	250.00	150.00	—
22.	Public-private partnership (capital nature—creating assets one time)	100.00	14,310.00	21.75
23.	Public-private partnership (revenue nature—recurring; maintenance)	20.00	20.00	17.23
	Total revenue expenditure	167,536.06	154,331.43	98,708.71
	Suspense heads (contra)			
1.	Basic Minimum Service	13.00	13.00	36.48
2.	National Slum Development Programme (NSDP)	1,000.00	1,000.00	2,187.73
3.	National Social Assistance Programme (NSAP)	500.00	400.00	652.48
4.	Kolkata Environmental Improvement Project (KEIP)	24,000.00	17,945.00	59.90

contd...

...contd...

S. No.	Particulars	Estimate 2008-09	Revised Estimate 2007-08	Actual Pre-Audited 2006-07
5.	Jawaharlal Nehru National Urban Renewal Mission (JNNURM)	28,000.00	2,420.00	151.54
6.	Department for International Development (DFID)	6,830.00	4,940.20	3,348.63
7.	MP Local Area Development Scheme (MPLAD)	4,000.00	3,200.00	3,126.63
8.	Bidhayak Elaka Unnayan Prakalpa (BEUP)	225.00	200.00	240.18
9.	Wage Employment Scheme	220.00	150.00	185.54
10.	Schemes under Ganga Action Plan	250.00	200.00	90.61
11.	Water Supply Programme for Mega City Plan	—	—	—
12.	Programme for installation of water meters	100.00	—	—
13.	Calcutta Urban Development Programme–III (Health)	50.00	50.00	71.84
14.	Valmiki Ambedkar Awas Yojana (VAMBAY) works (a GoI social housing scheme for the poor which provides for the construction of small quarters)	150.00	100.00	68.75
15.	Corpus fund (donations by NRIs for maintenance of historical monuments)	1,100.00	500.00	1.00
16.	Eleventh Finance Commission	—	200.00	1,045.27
17.	Twelfth Finance Commission	1,896.00	1,265.00	825.58
18.	State Finance Commission	1,698.00	1,133.00	1,114.11
19.	Non-convertible revenue bond	1,700.00	1,667.00	1,650.00
20.	Miscellaneous agencies	6,100.00	6,100.00	5,315.78
21.	Cost of work done in default	—	—	—
22.	Stores purchase	105.00	105.00	67.43
23.	Redevelopment of municipal market	50.00	175.00	147.84
24.	Deposit & advances to corporation employees	5,015.00	4,915.00	4,957.75
25.	Deposit & advances to contractors	7,530.00	7,530.00	10,473.89
26.	Short/medium-term loan	—	—	653.06
	Total contra heads (expenditure)	90,532.00	54,208.20	36,472.02
	Total revenue expenditure	167,536.06	154,331.43	98,708.71
	Total expenditure (revenue + suspense)	258,068.06	208,539.63	135,180.73

Source: Kolkata Municipal Corporation (2008a). Mayor's budget estimates for 2008-09.

6 Building Strong Local Governments

In this study a detailed assessment has been carried out of four municipal practices that have become the focus for strengthening local-level governance. The findings show that municipal institutions and urban residents are benefitting in several ways from these endeavours. For example, with the implementation of numerous legislative reforms, the marginalised groups and women are now getting the opportunity to participate in the municipal decision-making process. Elections are held regularly on the completion of a municipalities' term to constitute the next local body, and the financial base of numerous municipalities has improved with the constitution of State Finance Commissions (SFCs) and improved auditing of accounts. Similarly, capacity building activities are helping immensely in creating a sense of awareness among the municipal functionaries on the new approaches to good governance, about which they were completely ignorant. Due to this exposure, they are able to experiment with some innovative practices for providing improved civic services, and have been successful in generating additional funds for the council. e-Governance initiatives demonstrate the positive role played by technology in the delivery of basic civic services in large cities. Internet-based services have brought about a phenomenal increase in property tax paid, birth and death certificates issued, tenders processed, and the revenue generated against each service. In the projects on e-Governance, the private sector is playing an important role in providing technical expertise for software development and website maintenance. Lastly, financial reforms such as improvement in accounting and audit practices, issuance of bonds, revision in property tax assessment and collection procedures, monetisation of land, etc., have led to a sharp increase in municipal income. A sound financial base implies ability to undertake additional development and maintenance works.

The study also throws light on a number of problems in respect of the four practices reviewed, which are common to most Indian municipalities. These have been described in detail in the respective chapters, and may be broadly summed up as follows: (a) difficulties in implementing numerous legislative provisions, especially those relating to decentralisation of administration at the level of the ward and devolution of powers, functions, funds and functionaries from the state to municipal governments; (b) violation of municipal laws; strong opposition by the community/ functionaries at the time of revision of municipal taxes and promotion of public-private-partnerships (PPPs); (c) insufficient effect of capacity building programmes due to weak municipal resource base; (d) absence of e-Governance initiatives in several municipalities; (e) weak online grievance redressal mechanism and (f) slow progress in the implementation of modern financial practices.

Suggestions for Improving Local Government Performance

An important conclusion emerging from this study is that the reforms initiated to strengthen local government institutions (and to improve living conditions) have brought about only a marginal change and, that too, only in select Indian towns and cities. It indicates that, while it is realised that the reform measures have the ability to bring about marked improvements, there has been a failure in plumbing its full potential. Such problems often occur due to weak (or incomplete) governance strategies and poor (or careless) implementation and monitoring of various reforms. For example, if capacity building exercises are being conducted, it is necessary to understand how much their impact (in terms of success and/or failure) is on the functioning of the municipality and on the condition of the urban area, as also what kind of problems are being experienced by the trainers and the trainees. Based on lessons learnt, the methodology adopted to implement the initiative can be refined further in order to have a greater impact.

Evidently, further thinking and action are required to be undertaken for improving the performance of municipal agencies. A set of suggestions in respect of the four municipal practices reviewed in this study are listed below.

Effective Implementation and Enforcement of Laws

- Awareness programmes should be conducted for state/local government functionaries and the citizens on the significance of new legislative reforms, and the implementation guidelines; ongoing municipal capacity building programmes should be accordingly designed.
- Independent municipal law monitoring agencies should be created at the national and state levels to assist and guide the law enforcement agencies at the local level.
- A detailed study should be undertaken on the practices adopted by existing law enforcing agencies, which should review the powers, responsibilities and problems of legal officials affiliated with municipalities, availability of staff and infrastructure required for enforcement purposes, etc., in order to identify and address the constraints.
- Fines/penalties should be compulsorily imposed on any citizen/functionary found violating a municipal law.

Strengthening Capacity Building Efforts

- Additional training institutions should be established in each Indian state/UT so that all municipal functionaries get the opportunity to attend training programmes at regular intervals; funds for organising programmes should be made available from Central/state government sources, and from other national/international funding agencies. Some existing academic/research institutions in various states may be identified and involved in municipal capacity building.
- All municipal functionaries should be encouraged to attend training programmes regularly. The concerned departments at the state level (such as the Directorate of Local Bodies, etc.) should maintain time-series data on the number and category of participants by municipality.
- In some cases, arrangements should be made for organising training programmes within the premises of the local government, which will ensure higher participation of the municipal functionaries, and will save travel/accommodation-related costs.

- Select priority areas of training should be identified upon a detailed appraisal of local-level issues and availability of funds, for a greater impact of training and to minimise wastage of resources.
- There should be a proper follow-up of capacity building efforts in respect of each municipality by way of impact assessment.

Expansion of e-Governance Initiatives

- Hardware and (user-friendly) software requirements of municipalities should be fully addressed; supply of electricity in municipal offices should be improved.
- Municipal functionaries should be well-trained in the use of computers and software.
- Awareness programmes should be conducted for citizens on the advantages of using new technologies.
- Additional citizen service bureaus should be established for providing electronic services.
- Municipalities should build up a good reputation in the operation and maintenance of electronic services, especially in terms of addressing the complaints of citizens.

Augmenting Financial Base

- Transfer of funds from the Central and state government to local governments should take place without any delays; procedural bottlenecks should be identified and appropriately addressed.
- Fund requirements should be correctly estimated by the local bodies after giving due consideration to their functional domain and population projections, and by involving citizen's representatives.
- Greater transparency should be promoted in municipal finance practices; views of all municipal functionaries and citizens should be considered before spending funds on any development work.
- Expertise should be developed among municipal functionaries through capacity building programmes for optimal utilisation of funds received from the Centre and state government; programmes should give adequate importance to mobilisation of funds, financial management, levying new taxes, transfer of funds generated on

account of shared taxes, raising loans, budget formulation, enforcement of bye-laws, regular auditing of accounts, private sector participation in land and infrastructure development, regular enumeration of properties, etc.

- Costs incurred by local governments in the provision of civic services, such as water supply, sewerage, waste collection and disposal, etc., should be estimated accurately, and differential tax rates and service charges should be appropriately finalised in consultation with technical experts as well as citizen's representatives belonging to various income strata; municipal functionaries should be accordingly trained for this purpose; impact of efficient financial management on infrastructure and service delivery should be demonstrated to citizens for improved cost recovery.
- Municipal functionaries should be guided in the award of service contracts to local private operators for the operation and maintenance of various civic services. Such innovative practices will help in meeting the growing shortage of funds, equipment and manpower.

Furthermore, this study concludes that many of the bottlenecks to effective implementation of government's policy initiatives (such as JNNURM, 74th Amendment Act, etc.) may be done away with if the issues in local-level governance are comprehensively addressed. An empirical study (Aijaz, 2007) on the functioning of select municipalities in different Indian states reveals the presence of following issues at local government level, implying an enormous scope for the introduction of additional reforms.

Participation in the Decision-making Process

- Influence of social and economic factors on decision-making.
- Influence of political factors on decision-making.
- Ineffective women's participation in decision-making.
- Ignorance among elected members/authorities on Municipal Act provisions.

- Insufficient contribution of nominated and ex-officio members in decision-making.
- Dissatisfaction among several elected members regarding their participation in civic affairs.

Rule of Law and Transparency in the Conduct of Business

- Delays in convening municipal meetings.
- Violations in recording meeting minutes.
- Factionalism of elected members.
- Lack of transparency in sharing information on projects.
- Unfair practices in the publicity of development works.
- Discrimination in the selection of contractors, implying existence of corrupt practices.

Efficiency in Other Municipal Management and Finance Practices

- Bias against maintenance of existing infrastructure and services.
- Inefficiency in financial management (inappropriate pricing, low cost recovery, high outstanding dues, high dependence on Centre and state government, mismatch in income and expenditure accounts).
- Lack of coordination between local government, private contractors and *safai karamcharis* (i.e., sanitary workers) union; and between multiple civic agencies.
- Absence of citizen-local government interaction.

Equity at Ward Level

- Disparities in the level and quality of services available in wards.
- Inadequate attention given to service deficient wards.
- Absence of criteria for allocation of resources among wards.

Therefore, the study attempts to put forward the following additional suggestions for the governance of urban areas (Box 6.1).

The decentralised model for the governance of urban centres should be adopted. In this approach, the emphasis is on an appropriate delineation of authority/responsibility across levels of government. In the literature,

Box 6.1

Tasks for the Government to Improve Urban Governance

National and State Level

- Adoption of a decentralised approach: clearer delineation of powers and functions across levels of government; popular participation
- Study of ULGI performance and problems by independent academic institutions
- Adequate support and directions to ULGIs (funds, personnel, expertise, technology, training, etc.)
- National and state political parties in power to ensure higher representation in ULGIs by formulating strategies based on good governance principles
- Election Commission to ensure fairness and transparency in conduct of municipal elections
- Greater popular participation in governance and development

Local Level

- Formulation of a Urban Development Plan (UDP); plan to be implemented by adopting a partnership approach
- Study of ULGI performance and problems by independent local academic institutions
- Vital statistics, annual report and best practices to be made available online at municipal website
- Introduction of a performance appraisal system in ULGIs
- Ranking of wards based on existing infrastructure and service levels
- Constitution of well-equipped and representative ward-level governing entities

decentralisation[1] is regarded as a prerequisite for good governance because the process helps in producing 'more efficient and equitable service delivery through making better use of local knowledge, leads to greater participation and democracy, greater accountability, and more responsive and responsible government' (Estache, 1995). The most common rationale for

1. Decentralisation, as the term implies, is a process which involves a transfer of responsibilities for financing, allocating, planning and managing resources from Central government to entities operating at local levels.

decentralisation is that: 'the needs of citizens can best be addressed by those entities that are located closest to them; expansive administrative responsibilities cannot be carried out by central governments alone; socio-economic progress requires people's active participation; resource mobilisation necessitates local initiatives; and devolution of power is a pre-condition for a democratic mode of governance' (Haque, 1997).

All the three tiers of government—Centre, state and local—should continue to play a role in urban governance. The existence of multiple entities (or popular participation in the governance process), including the parastatal agencies, the local government, private operators and various civil society organisations, should be seen as an asset and not a liability.

The role, powers, responsibilities and functions of each government entity should be reviewed thoroughly, and necessary institutional and administrative reforms may be carried out to eliminate any overlaps in the functional/power domain, so that there is a clearer division in the role played and tasks handled by each entity.

The Centre and state-level entities should offer adequate support (in the form of funds, personnel, expertise, technology, training, etc.), guidance and directions for the efficient functioning of local government institutions, and abstain from handling the day-to-day civic functions. The nature of support to be provided by the Centre and state should be based on a careful and detailed assessment/study of the problems experienced by the local government institutions and the grievances of the municipal functionaries. This goal should also be addressed by undertaking capacity building programmes to broaden the knowledge base of municipal functionaries.

Urban local government institution (ULGI)/municipality should be the main agency responsible for all matters concerning urban governance. This suggestion is based on the fact that the Municipal Acts empower ULGIs to function in a fully democratic manner, which is not the case with other entities engaged in urban governance. In this respect, a reference may be made to the existing form and composition of ULGI in India (Box 6.2). The municipal laws allow representatives of citizens (i.e., councillors) from various sections of the society to participate in the decision-making process. Councillors are in close contact with the citizens, unlike other elected leaders such as MPs and MLAs, and possess in-depth knowledge of the development profile of wards, including the day-to-day civic problems experienced by the ward residents. Furthermore, the councillors possess powers to accept or reject decisions on various municipal matters discussed during municipal meetings. Thus, local governments would benefit enormously if knowledge of elected councillors is judiciously utilised in the planning, execution, implementation and maintenance of ward-level schemes.

An essential task for the political parties in power at the national and state level should be to ensure that a sizeable proportion of persons affiliated to their party are elected to the post of councillors in local governments. In most cities/urban areas this objective has not been achieved. Thus, one political party is more influential at local government level, and often there is clash of interest with councillors from the opposition party which is in minority, as well as with elected members of state government (or the state government functionaries) who belong to a different political party. To overcome such problems, party workers already affiliated with the local government (or the political party itself) should formulate a fair, long-term strategy based on good governance principles with achievable targets for winning confidence among the masses. They should fulfill all the promises made at the time of contesting in elections insofar as the development of their wards is concerned, and be accountable to the citizens who have elected them and vested their faith in them, in order to set a good example.

Another important fundamental requirement of democratic governance is to ensure fairness and transparency in the conduct of municipal elections, including accuracy in the compilation of a voter's list (or enumeration of voters) and in the voting process managed by the election commission. Such initiatives would help greatly in paving the way for legitimate persons to win seats during municipal elections, and in overcoming the problems of coordination experienced by the national, state or the local government for a long time, and would also improve institutional accountability.

A realistic short-term and well-structured urban development plan (UDP) addressing current and future needs of towns and cities should be formulated by the municipality with the assistance and involvement of all the concerned government departments/urban and regional development

Box 6.2

Form of Urban Local Government Institution (ULGI) in India

Municipal corporations in India are structured according to the pattern described in the Bombay Municipal Corporations Act of 1888. An important characteristic of this pattern is the separation of deliberative and executive functions of the corporation. In this system, the municipal commissioner, who is a state government appointed official, is the executive authority of the corporation and is entrusted with the responsibility of controlling the entire administrative machinery. The mayor and other elected members associated with the ULGI, who are representatives of citizens, on the other hand, look after the deliberative responsibilities—laying down broad policies, framing bye-laws, sanctioning municipal budget, etc.

With the enactment of the Constitution (74th Amendment) Act, 1992 that paves the way for the empowerment of Indian municipalities, ULGIs are now well representative bodies. These comprise elected (i.e., mayor, councillors), nominated (i.e., select persons having knowledge/experience in municipal administration) and ex-officio members (i.e., MPs, MLAs), as well as government appointed authorities (i.e., commissioner, other officials and staff).

Elections to ULGIs are held periodically in which seats for the posts of mayor and councillors are reserved for women as well as scheduled castes/tribes and backward classes in order to protect their interests. Cities/urban areas in India are divided into smaller administrative units (namely wards) in such a manner that the population in each ward is kept the same, as far as possible. There is a contest for the seat/post of councillor/ward representative in municipalities from among the eligible voters at the ward level and one person from each ward is elected to the post of councillor.

Decisions on all municipal matters (including superintendence of municipal administration, development of infrastructure facilities, approval of municipal budget, etc.) are taken during the meetings of local government usually held once a month. During a meeting, resolutions [formal statement of a committee's opinion] are passed on the basis of voting. The group of persons participating in this event may include the elected, nominated and ex-officio members, and other appointed authorities/officers associated with the local government.

contd...

...*contd*...

However, decisions to accept or reject resolutions are taken only by the elected members (councillors, mayor[2]) who possess powers for voting. For this reason, the elected members (who are representatives of citizens associated with the local government) are important actors engaged in the decision-making process.

Accepted resolutions are implemented only under the supervision of the government appointed commissioner, who possesses executive powers. The role of other participants is to provide assistance on various technical, financial and legal matters.

Source: Aijaz (2008).

authorities and citizen groups, and implemented by adopting a community/ private sector participation approach. There should be sufficient scope for involvement of citizen's representatives in deciding on expenditure meant for carrying out development work within wards. At present, residents neither have a say nor do they know how councillors decide on the allocation of funds. For controlling the adverse impacts of market forces (i.e., real estate sector) on urban development, a favourable regulatory and monitoring environment should be created by the government. Any development activity to be carried out should be as per the plan proposals, and with prior approval of the municipality. In addition to recommendations on various urban planning components (such as shelter, infrastructure, services, heritage, environment, trade and commerce, land use, etc.) and the avenues for resource mobilisation, the plan should clearly spell out and meet the defined norms/standards for various civic infrastructure and services at the regional, town/city, and the ward level.

The Central and state governments should engage local research/ academic institutions for studying the performance and problems of ULGIs (and their functionaries) in the country on a yearly basis based on uniform indicators, including their resource requirements (such as funds,

2. The power to vote for a resolution lies only with the councillor. The other members and authorities who participate in the meeting do not have liberty to vote upon or to make any proposition at such meetings. However, in case of an equality of votes, the mayor has the right of casting vote.

equipment, personnel and expertise), and accordingly provide the necessary support and reform guidelines. The ULGIs should fully cooperate with the local research institutions in the sharing of data/information on various civic matters. An effort should also be made to improve transparency in municipal management and finance practices as well as statistics maintained in the municipal offices by uploading such information, data and reports on the municipal websites.

A performance appraisal system should be introduced to assess the functioning of various municipal sub-committees (namely finance, health and sanitation, public works and buildings, tax assessment, etc.). Yearly appraisal of achievements *vis à vis* targets set at the beginning of the financial year should be carried out by a well represented evaluation committee. This will ensure higher levels of efficiency, transparency and accountability at the local government level.

The wards in towns and cities should be ranked on the basis of existing levels of civic infrastructure and services, and accordingly funds should be released for their development. The policy should be to allocate more funds to those wards which show lower levels of development. This would help in the reduction of intra-urban disparities.

Well-equipped and representative ward-level governing entities should be established by the municipality. The staff working in these units should be made responsible for collecting and maintaining vital statistics on ward-level infrastructure and services, and provide various civic services on a day-to-day basis to the ward residents.

For the efficient governance of large urban centres, it is necessary to ensure that good coordination prevails between the multiple institutions that function at the local level. Quite often as a result of lack of coordination, many of the city modernisation plans have suffered a setback. This is noted in the case of Delhi, the capital of India, which is governed by the Union and Delhi government, and several Centre, state and local entities such as the Office of the Lieutenant Governor (LG), Delhi Development Authority (DDA), Public Works Department (PWD), Delhi Police, Municipal Corporation of Delhi (MCD), New Delhi Municipal Council (NDMC), Delhi Cantonment Board, etc. Even though the responsibilities of each entity are fairly distinct, due to various reasons there is a tendency among the functionaries to disagree on those matters where the action of one entity affects the jurisdiction of the other. For instance, the implementation of a road widening project involving removal of trees initiated by MCD was delayed because the environment department of the Delhi government was not in favour of causing damage to the natural landscape. Another conflicting issue is related to the proposed revision of circle rates[3] by the Delhi government for the colonies and localities in Delhi. The circle rate of properties is a system used by the government to fix the minimum rate of the land/property depending on the category of colony it falls in. The initiative attempts to address the concern of loss of state revenues (amounting to about Rs 30 million daily) due to undervaluation of properties, and black money circulation in property transactions. This move was opposed by the office of the LG on the grounds that the proposed 100 per cent hike in rate structure for all the eight categories of colonies is not favourable to the common man. Accordingly, a realistic rate structure was recommended by the LG with higher circle rates in colonies where land is expensive and lower rates in areas where land is cheaper. The issue was finally resolved by the Union Home Ministry which maintained that the subject of circle rates falls under the transferred list of subjects and hence the LG has to act with the aid and advice of the states' council of ministers. Similarly, there is frequent adjournment of MCD house over petty issues. On one occasion, the Standing Committee chairperson was not allowed to present the Budget because the Congress party councillors accused the BJP-led MCD for misleading the people. Such problems of coordination have continued to prevail over the years, and hence most functionaries view multiplicity of authorities as a major bottleneck in the way of planned growth of Delhi.

Some steps have been undertaken in Delhi to deal with the problems of coordination. However, the recent efforts have failed to bring about the desired change in quality of urban life. The initiative of the Delhi government to gain control over MCD (under the Union Ministry of Home Affairs) and DDA (under the Union Ministry of Urban Development) is justified from the point of view that whenever something goes wrong, it is

3. Minimum rates for valuation of land and immovable properties for purposes of registration under the Registration Act, 1908; the rates were first introduced in 2007, and for this purpose the city was divided into eight categories from A to H.

the Delhi government that has to answer to the people of the capital. It is also emphasised that such measures would improve accountability in the execution of various development projects. For this reason, there is a demand for transferring all civic powers and functions to a single entity, namely the Delhi government (GoNCT of Delhi, 2006). The proposal of the Delhi government has been partly accepted by the Union Home Ministry, which issued a notification for the devolution of some civic and financial powers and legislative provisions of the MCD Act, 1957, and some powers in possession of the LG, including review of MCD performance, making building bye-laws, implementing zonal plans, allocation of Central government funds, issue of directions concerning MCD schools, salary of commissioner, etc. Though the move allows Delhi government to control a part of MCD functioning, major decisions including the dissolution of MCD and appointment of the commissioner still requires approval of the Centre. Besides, some powers continue to remain with the LG.

Thus, many government policy reforms, aimed at improving the quality of life in large cities of India and on which huge investments are made, often fail in achieving their objectives because sufficient attention is not given to the issues of coordination. This could also be a significant reason for the partial success of the reform measures reviewed in this study, namely revision of laws, capacity building, e-Governance and financial management. In this respect, the study makes the point that the current thrust by the Centre on strengthening of ULGIs must be accompanied by suitable actions to deal with the problems of coordination in order to have a better impact of any new initiative. Such reforms would help in the judicious utilisation of funds and other scarce resources required for creating habitable cities.

Policy analysts are concerned about the connection between the various institutional coordination issues and the impact of reforms. However, as observed in the case of Delhi, finding an amicable solution to this problem is proving to be a complex and challenging task. The functioning of the three tiers of the government (*viz.*, Centre, state and local) based on democratic principles is absolutely necessary, but it is also common knowledge that such arrangements have given birth to numerous coordination issues. In this form of governance, a clash of interests among the elected leaders affiliated to various national-level political parties as well as the bureaucracy is quite common. Such problems have intricate political dimensions and vested interests, and call for a need to evolve novel policy directions. As mentioned earlier, implementing a truly decentralised approach (based on democratic and good governance principles) to city/urban governance would be useful in addressing the coordination-related problems.

Novel Governance Practices in India

This study has described the impact and shortcomings of select recent initiatives of the Indian government implemented as part of the country's urban development reform process. In this section, information is provided on several novel governance practices observed in various parts of India which have made a mark in addressing complex urban problems.

Mayor-in-Council

In the existing form of municipal administration, the mayor, who is the holder of the highest civic office, does not possess executive powers for governance. It is widely argued that policy and administration are inextricably intertwined and the two should not be handled by different authorities, namely the elected representatives and the appointed officials. Therefore, some state governments (including Maharashtra and West Bengal) took the initiative to remodel the administrative structure of ULGIs. In the new arrangement (known as Mayor-in-Council), the executive power is vested in the mayor and the council of elected representatives, while the municipal commissioner functions under the supervision and control of the mayor, and is responsible for providing assistance in administrative matters.[4] Thus, the mayor and the council play a more active role in policy formulation as well as in executive matters.

An appraisal of the new governance framework showed mixed results in terms of its existence. Kolkata continues to display a strong 'mayoral concept' since mid-eighties, whereas in Nagpur and Mumbai, the system was subsequently withdrawn.

---

4. Kolkata Municipal Corporation: *https://www.kmcgov.in/KMCPortal/HomeAction.do*

Participatory Governance

There is growing evidence of municipal governments engaged in partnerships with private operators and the community.

In the urban water supply and sanitation sector, service contracts have been awarded to private operators in centres such as Chandrapur, Chennai, Jamshedpur, Mysore, Nagpur, Navi Mumbai, Rajkot and Surat. By involving the private sector, the civic agencies are said to be benefitting in terms of cost savings and better performance. The 24/7 water supply project initiated by Nagpur Municipal Corporation (Maharashtra) in PPP mode has helped in increasing supply from 4 to 24 hours, and increasing pressure received at consumer taps from 2-5 metres to 10-12 metres thereby resulting in energy saving for consumers.[5] In the same manner, Alandur municipality (Tamil Nadu) successfully provided underground sewerage system to all residents including the urban poor.

In Tirupur town, which accounts for a sizeable proportion of India's cotton knitwear exports, the state government involved the private sector in urban development with the aim of expanding production and generating opportunities for investment and employment. For this purpose, a Tirupur Area Development Programme (TADP) was jointly designed by the Tamil Nadu Corporation for Industrial Infrastructure Development Limited—TACID (formed by the Government of Tamil Nadu), Tirupur Exporters Association, and Infrastructure Leasing and Financial Services (IL&FS) (a private company). Technical assistance and training for the successful implementation of the programme was provided under the Financial Institutions' Reform and Expansion Programme[6] of the United States Agency for International Development (USAID). To implement TADP, a public limited company (namely New Tirupur Area Development Corporation Limited) was established in 1995 to develop, construct, operate and maintain a 185 million litre per day capacity water supply project and sewerage facility for about 60 per cent population, as well as

5. National Urban Water Awards: *http://www.waterawards.in/*
6. The programme is designed to support the development of commercially viable infrastructure finance system through the development of debt market. It aims at lending support to the Government of India in its effort to revamp India's capital markets to enable them to serve as efficient and reliable sources of development finance.

provision of low cost sanitation facilities in slums. The participation of the state government, a private finance company, the exporters association and principal beneficiaries in the financing and implementation of the urban infrastructure development programme is observed as a unique experiment in the country.[7]

The Bangalore Agenda Task Force (BATF), constituted by a state government order in November 1999, works with various city-level civic agencies to deal with the development problems arising from rapid urbanisation. It is represented by prominent citizens and government functionaries. The main objective is to offer advice to the city stakeholders in achieving their targets, and undertake projects (on road infrastructure, public health and sanitation, fund-based accounting system, etc.) in partnership with the stakeholders with the aim of demonstrating good practices. To improve efficiency in operation, BATF involves the corporate sector, IT firms and specialists. According to an independent opinion poll conducted by a reputed agency, the city has experienced noticeable improvement in governance practices and infrastructure levels.

Furthermore, community and government-led initiatives to improve living conditions are quite common.

Sulabh International Social Service Organisation (SISSO), founded in 1970 as a voluntary non-profit organisation, works for the liberation of scavengers from the sub-human practice of manual excreta cleaning, and improvement of sanitary conditions. The major activities undertaken by the organisation include: conversion of dry household latrines into new pour-flush toilets; construction of public toilets and wash areas; retraining scavengers in the maintenance of new latrines; educating the community about public health; development of technology to make biogas plant effluents free from colour, odour and pathogens; development of technology for composting of biodegradable wastes, and for waste water treatment.[8] Sulabh's work is widely recognised at the national and international level, and besides India, their technology is in use in some developing countries.

---

7. New Tirupur Area Development Corporation Limited: *http://www.ilfsindia.com/group_co.asp?gmchild=7*

8. Sulabh International Social Service Organisation: *http://www.sulabhinternational.org/*

ExNoRa International, founded in Chennai in 1989, is a citizen-led movement focussing on clean surroundings. The NGO motivates and involves people in the sanitation of their area not only in Chennai but also in some districts of Tamil Nadu, Karnataka, Andhra Pradesh and Kerala. Till date, about 5,000 community-based organisations (called Civic ExNoRas) have been formed for the purpose of waste management, which cover about 30,000 streets and settlements.[9] In addition, ExNoRa is engaged in liquid waste management, rain water harvesting, waste recycling, and organising lectures and demonstrations to generate awareness among the society about environmental problems.

The Government of National Capital Territory (NCT) of Delhi initiated a 'Bhagidari' (i.e., partnership) Programme in January 2000. Through this programme, an attempt is being made to resolve various problems faced by residents living in Delhi, such as water shortage and pipe leakages, chocked sewers, power shortage and faulty electricity meters, solid waste heaps, broken roads and lanes, poor maintenance of parks, traffic congestion, crime, encroachments, slums, grievances related to collection and payment of taxes, issue of licences, sales tax, weights and measurements used for commercial purposes, etc. To achieve this task, various departments of the Delhi government are working in partnership with a number of citizen groups. This is due to the realisation that successful and meaningful governance cannot be achieved without the involvement of citizens. In this approach, the citizen groups and government officials meet, sit together, interact, overcome their inhibitions, and develop a real dialogue, to act together and solve problems together. Frequent workshops are held during which issues are discussed, solutions are identified and steps are taken towards implementation. This is followed by monthly reviews of the progress by departmental heads and deputy commissioners; quarterly reviews by chief secretary and steering committee headed by the chief minister. A 'Bhagidari' cell has been created in the chief minister's office for the coordination of activities, and the general administration department functions as a nodal agency to provide financial and administrative support. To involve more people, a decentralised approach is being

9. Exnora International: *http://www.exnora.org/*

followed, wherein at the revenue district level, deputy commissioner (revenue) operates as district coordinator. Currently, more than 2,000 citizen groups are a part of the programme.[10] The important achievements under the scheme include participation of a large number of resident welfare associations (RWAs) and market and traders associations in the following activities: collective payment of water bills, observing and reporting water leakages, distribution of water through tankers, undertaking rain water harvesting measures, replacement of old water pipes, street lighting improvement, implementation of tree plantation projects, and creating awareness against use of plastic bags.

Urban Development Funds

In some states of India, financial arrangements have been made to enable municipal governments, statutory boards and private corporations borrow funds for implementing a wide range of infrastructure projects. For example, the Tamil Nadu Urban Development Fund (TNUDF) was created in 1988 under the Tamil Nadu Urban Development Project (TNUDP). The fund, which provides debt finance to borrowers on a non-guarantee basis, has been put in place by adopting a PPP approach, wherein the state government has entered into a partnership with three all-India financial institutions, namely Industrial Credit and Investment Corporation of India (ICICI), Infrastructure Development Finance Company (IDFC) and IL&FS. The state government's equity in the venture is restricted to 49 per cent, in order to facilitate private sector management in investment decisions. This facility allows interested agencies to borrow funds up to a maximum of 90 per cent of the cost of the project, provided they demonstrate efficiency in financial management, and possess adequate institutional capacity to implement projects on water supply, sanitation, roads, transportation, sites and services, area development, etc.[11]

Lessons Learned

With the adoption of novel governance practices, some urban governments have been partly successful in offering an improved quality of life to the citizens. For instance, the capacity building initiative has helped

---

10. Bhagidari programme: *http://www.delhigovt.nic.in/bhagi.asp*
11. Tamil Nadu Urban Development Fund: *http://www.tnudf.com/index.asp*

in generation of income by the municipality and in improving the urban area. The Centre, state government and external agencies such as the USAID have provided the much needed financial support and technical expertise. Moreover, the training institute in Nainital is sufficiently equipped to conduct training programmes. The same level of success will not be achieved in states lacking in suitable training facilities and funds. Similarly, enormous funds and technology required for implementing e-Governance projects can be made available by encouraging partnerships between the public and private sector, as observed in the case of Delhi. Also, the study shows that the civic agency in Kolkata has gradually shown improvement in its revenue base. This was possible only by implementing improved financial practices, such as accounting and auditing, property tax reforms, and PPPs in the development of land, infrastructure and markets.

It would also be useful to understand the reasons behind the emergence of such reforms. Insofar as the four practices (namely revision of laws, capacity building, e-Governance and financial management) are concerned, the Indian government realises that such measures will help in improving the performance of civic agencies and the urban areas. Hence, these are mandatory reforms to be implemented by the state and local governments, and for this purpose necessary financial, technical and institutional support is being offered under the JNNURM. Other innovative reforms have occurred at the initiative of the state/local governments, civil society, financial institutions (HUDCO, LIC), external support agencies (ADB, DFID, JBIC, UN, USAID, World Bank), since many of these are either exploring ways to exhibit a greater degree of efficiency, accountability and transparency in their functioning, or have a mandate to offer support, or are concerned about the deteriorating living conditions. Some important examples are the Mayor-in-Council (Kolkata), popular participation (Bengaluru, Tirupur), involvement of private operators in a large number of urban centres, robust leadership (Surat). In certain instances, the initiative is either led by the community (Sulabh; PROUD, Mumbai; ExNoRa, Chennai; Swabhiman movement, Bengaluru; Express Group of Citizens, Pune; Citizen Report Cards) or the government (citizen's charter; Bhagidari, Delhi). Every initiative has demonstrated a positive impact, and at the same time, new challenges are being encountered by the stakeholders.

With increasing emphasis on creating opportunities to showcase/share best practices, there is immense possibility of urban governments benefitting from such reform measures.[12] A challenging task, however, for the nation is their widespread occurrence, since most are visible in large cities where governments are much more capable, the private sector is dynamic and, the civil society is well informed. The effective implementation of municipal capacity building initiatives might help to some extent in achieving such an important objective.

A noteworthy observation, nevertheless, is the emergence of new forms of governance based on certain fundamental principles. This line of thinking has also received considerable impetus from the contribution made by the UN-Habitat (Box 6.3), which defines urban governance as the 'sum of the many ways individuals and institutions, public and private, plan and manage the common affairs of the city'.

Box 6.3

A Model of Urban Governance

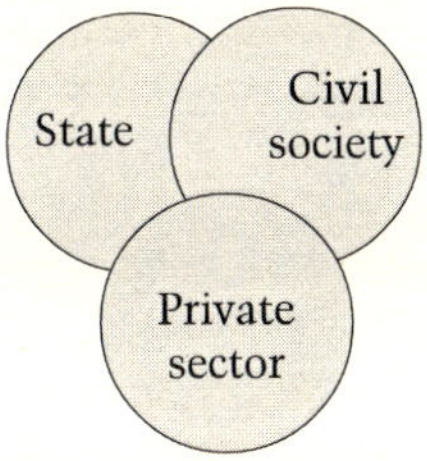

- Governance includes the state, but transcends it by taking in the private sector and civil society.
- All three are critical for sustaining human development. The state creates a conducive political and legal environment. The private sector generates jobs and income. And civil society facilitates political and social interaction —mobilising groups to participate in economic, social and political activities.
- Because each has weaknesses and strengths, the objective should be to promote constructive interaction among all three.

Source: UNDP (1997).

12. UN Habitat best practices database: *http://www.bestpractices.org/*; UN Habitat India: *http://www.unchs.org/categories.asp?catid=46* ; World Bank India: *http://www.worldbank.org.in/WBSITE/EXTERNAL/COUNTRIES/SOUTHASIAEXT/INDIAEXTN/0,,menuPK:295589~pagePK:141159~piPK:141110~theSitePK:295584,00.html*

As part of UN efforts, numerous campaigns on good urban governance have been launched from time to time in collaboration with governments of many countries including India.[13] The principles are formulated with the intention of ensuring the voices of the poorest and the vulnerable in decision-making over the allocation of development resources. An important recommendation is to develop an understanding on urban governance within the framework of democratic or good governance norms (Table 6.1).

Table 6.1

Norms of Good Urban Governance

S. No.	*Norm*	*Description of Norm*
1	Participation	All men and women should have a voice in decision-making, either directly or through legitimate intermediate institutions that represent their interest. Local democracy and decentralisation are pre-requisites for participation.
2	Strategic vision	Leaders and the public should have a broad and long-term perspective on good governance, human development and the development of their city along with a sense of what is needed for such development.
3	Rule of law	Legal frameworks should be fair and enforced impartially, particularly the law on human rights.
4	Transparency	Processes, institutions and information are directly accessible to all stakeholders, and enough information is provided to understand and monitor the governance process.
5	Responsiveness	Institutions and processes try to serve all stakeholders.
6	Consensus orientation	Different interests are mediated in order to reach a broad consensus on what is the best interest of the group, and where possible on policies and procedures.
7	Equity/equity building	All men and women have opportunities to improve or maintain their well-being; equity of access to decision-making processes and the basic necessities of urban life.
8	Effectiveness and efficiency	Processes and institutions produce results that meet needs while making the best use of resources; efficiency in the delivery of public services and in promoting local economic development.
9	Accountability	Decision-makers in government, the private sector and civil society organisations are accountable to the public, as well as to institutional stakeholders.

Source: Etten and Dool (2001).

13. The India Campaign for Good Urban Governance was launched on 3 September 2001.

Popular Approaches for Achieving Good Governance in Developing Countries

To deal with the problems being experienced in the governance of urban areas, innovative approaches are being adopted in various parts of the world. An important observation in this respect is a change in the role of governments. From a traditional 'provider' of services, governments are beginning to act more as 'facilitators'. Under this new arrangement, actors outside the public sector, such as private agencies, community groups, etc., are being enabled to participate in and contribute to the governance process.

A survey of literature shows that governments at some places have created autonomous or semi-autonomous authorities, also known as parastatal organisations, to which some of the functions are entrusted. Parastatal organisations are owned and controlled in most cases by the government and are often formed for their support. In many countries, these entities have been reformed to achieve greater efficiency and accountability through commercialisation (agencies are given separate budgets and financial autonomy based on tariff revenues, and managerial autonomy to operate as a business) and corporatisation (agencies are transformed into a legal entity subject to company law, with formal separation of ownership and management responsibility). In Kenya, for example, municipalities of Kericho, Eldoret and Nyeri were allowed to form companies and enter into contracts under the local government act. Major cities in several countries of the world have experienced the advantages and effectiveness of putting in place a public service corporation-type of authority for the collection, transfer and disposal of a municipality's solid waste.

Decentralisation

Governments of several countries, traditionally characterised by centralised systems of governance, have shown a move towards decentralisation. According to this approach, local entities (such as the local government) have been increasingly empowered (administratively, politically and financially) to play an active role in the delivery of urban services.

The form and extent of decentralisation varies across countries. In parts of Africa, local political entities have been created. In Eastern Europe, existing local administrative units of the Central governments have been transformed into separate political entities, with its leadership chosen through elections. Similarly, in Latin America, there has been a shift from centrally appointed mayors to locally elected mayors, as well as major increases in inter-governmental fiscal transfers.

An example of decentralisation in the infrastructure sector is observed in the case of South Africa, where the government embarked on a decentralisation programme. The old system of governance in the water and sanitation sector was characterised by strong centralisation of control and responsibility. The main factors of the old system included setting of rules and regulations at the Central level and provision of services through a combination of government departments, public water boards and municipalities. Moreover, public inputs into decision-making at all levels were virtually missing. The key features of new reforms undertaken are listed below:

- devolution of responsibility for provision of water and sanitation services to individual municipalities, which include an element of public consultation and planning;
- clarification of functions and objectives of regional water boards and
- strengthening managerial and technical capacity of municipalities, in view of their enhanced responsibilities.

Indonesia is another example where the government initiated a nationwide programme of decentralising the planning and implementation responsibilities of urban infrastructure projects to local governments. In 1985, the Indonesian government embarked upon a new Integrated Urban Infrastructure Development Programme (IUIDP) to change past practices, which were characterised by centralised power and funds. In this context, the Central government's new role was perceived as that of an 'enabler' rather than a 'provider' of all resources and services. The IUIDP has the following key features:

- decentralisation of responsibility for planning, programming, budgeting and implementation of urban services delivery to local governments;

- strengthening the local governments capacity to mobilise resources for infrastructure development and
- emphasis on multisectoral, medium-term investment programming.

The IUIDP approach places greater and new responsibilities for all actors that are involved. In support of this, a training and communication programme has been developed to prepare staff at all levels. The broad fields of training include engineering, strategic planning, programming, project implementation, financial management and project administration.

Participation

Participation is yet another approach that has consistently gained recognition and is argued by many as crucial to good urban governance. In the past, governance practices have been characterised by the participation of the community and the private sector. More recently, emphasis is being laid on promoting popular participation (or public-private community partnership). The underlying argument in this regard is that good urban governance will occur only with the active support and participation of national, provincial/state and city governments as well as other actors from the community and the private sector.

Community Participation

An appraisal of case studies demonstrates that in a number of developing countries, innovative forms of participatory mechanisms have evolved to improve access for urban communities to basic services (Table 6.2). For example, at Villa El Salvador in Lima (Peru), which was a relocated low-income settlement with virtually no facilities, three levels of organisation (i.e., household, block and settlement) were created from within the community. Each level was made responsible for certain functions of management and service provision. The government, as partner and facilitator, provided trunk services, social and community development support, and access to building materials. Within a period of five years, the self-managed efforts of the people made El Salvador a well-organised settlement with water and electricity connections, street lighting, a community-run bank, basic health facilities, etc. In Somolu, a metropolitan area of Lagos (Nigeria), the local authority embraced democratic management practices to set right the deteriorating condition of

Table 6.2

Main Features of Community Participation Strategies

Item Description	*Strategy/Form of Participation*			
	Community-based Support Strategy[14]	*Area-based Involvement Strategy*[15]	*Function-based Collaboration Strategy*[16]	*Process-based Decentralisation Strategy*[17]
Strategic basis	Social group or community	Residential area	Service delivery functions	Infrastructure management process
Objective of participation	Support and enable self-managed infrastructure development by user communities	Involve users in government-directed infrastructure development programmes to improve their effectiveness	Collaborate with user and community groups on the basis of clear and coordinated division of tasks and responsibilities	Decentralise management functions to improve demand-responsiveness
Orientation of partnership	Government (and NGO) inputs to community-based development	User inputs to government-directed processes of infrastructure development	Coordinated, self-managed activities of various stakeholders	User and citizen inputs into government-based infrastructure management processes
Scope of participatory management	• Implementation	• Programming • Implementation • Operation and maintenance	• Planning • Programming • Implementation • Operation and maintenance	• Policymaking • Planning • Programming • Implementation • Operation and maintenance • Monitoring and evaluation

contd...

14. In a community-based support approach, government agencies provide assistance in meeting the demands raised by the community.
15. The difference between the community-based support strategy and an area-based involvement strategy is that in the latter, the community is mobilised to participate/contribute towards a government-managed activity.
16. The function-based collaboration strategy is quite similar to the earlier mentioned involvement strategy except that the local people are not only involved in government-directed infrastructure development process, but they also assume full responsibility for self-management and the self-financing of a limited portion of the infrastructure systems.
17. There are two distinguishing features that differentiate this approach with the previously mentioned approaches. First, people participate in the entire process of infrastructure service management (i.e., in policymaking, planning, programming, implementation, operation and maintenance, monitoring and evaluation). Second, to enable this participation, the decision-making and management functions, which in most instances are under the control of the Central government/higher authorities, are decentralised (transferred) to the local governments and to the communities.

...contd...

Item Description	*Strategy/Form of Participation*			
	Community-based Support Strategy	*Area-based Involvement Strategy*	*Function-based Collaboration Strategy*	*Process-based Decentralisation Strategy*
Examples	• Government-supported self-managed development: Villa El Salvador, Lima (Peru) • PROFAVELA Pilot Project: São Paulo (Brazil) • Naga City Participatory Planning Initiative: Philippines	• Kampung Improvement Programme: Indonesia • Participatory Action Planning: Somolu (Nigeria)	• Orangi Pilot Project: Karachi (Pakistan) • Community-managed local Garbage Collection: Indonesia	• Million Houses Programme: Sri Lanka

Source: Schubeler (1996).

civic services. After a decade of 'top-down' planning and weak implementation, it was realised that living conditions in low-income settlements could be improved only by involving the community in the decision-making process and through their participation in consultative meetings. By adopting this strategy, significant progress was achieved in road rehabilitation, extension of water supply and drainage facilities, etc. Furthermore, the community associations were also involved in the operation and maintenance of services. The civil society in Naga city (Central Philippines) works closely with the local government to design, implement and evaluate the city's development agenda. Thus, consultations at the village, city and task force levels are held, strategic management plans are prepared and the City Health Board has been rehabilitated.

Private Sector Participation

Private sector participation is increasingly becoming a key feature in economic structural reforms in developing countries. Many governments have considered this approach as a way to address the deficiencies in urban infrastructure and services (Table 6.3).

Table 6.3

Main Features of Privatisation Strategies

Item Description	*Strategy/Form of Private Sector Participation*					
	Service Contract[18]	*Management Contract*[19]	*Lease Contract*[20]	*Concession Contract*[21]	*Joint Venture*[22]	*Divestiture/ Outright Sale*[23]
System operation and maintenance						
System management						
Financing of working capital						
Financing of investments						
Ownership of assets						

contd...

18. When the government (public authority) enters into a contract agreement with private operators to provide goods and services or to manage certain service-related activities, the practice is termed as a service contract.
19. In a management contract, the responsibility of the private sector is extended beyond individual service functions and often includes the entire operation and maintenance of the system.
20. Lease contracts are arrangements in which a private contractor is involved to play a larger role in service delivery. The public authority grants exclusive rights to the contractor to operate, maintain and manage the system, in return of which a rental or licence fee is charged.
21. In a concession contract, the private company contracts with the government to build or expand and operate an infrastructure system. This particular feature, in which the private company is also engaged in financing capital investments for the expansion of services, differentiates concessions from lease contracts.
22. In a joint venture, the public authority and the private entity share the ownership and control of infrastructure. This arrangement is different from a service or lease contract, in that the private sector is allowed to maintain a relatively higher degree of participation. It is also different from a concession contract, in that the full responsibility for investment and operation is not awarded to the private operator due to associated risks, especially during the initial stages of a sector reform programme.
23. When the public sector sells infrastructure systems including its ownership shares to the private sector, the arrangement is termed as divestiture. The public sector benefits from the revenue raised in this manner. For the private buyer, the main attraction is the rates they are permitted to charge, since installations have negligible alternative value.

...contd...

Item Description	*Strategy/Form of Private Sector Participation*					
	Service Contract	*Management Contract*	*Lease Contract*	*Concession Contract*	*Joint Venture*	*Divestiture/ Outright Sale*
Duration (in years)	1-2	3-5	5-10	20-30	According to contract	Perpetuity
Sectors in which used	Water supply, sewerage, solid waste, railways, roads	Water supply, sanitation, power	Water supply, sanitation, power, ports, transport, railways	Power, water supply, solid waste, ports, railways, metro systems, toll roads, telecom	Airlines, railways, telecom, solid waste	Water supply, telecom, airlines, electricity, port, transport
Examples	Santiago (Chile), Kuala Lumpur (Malaysia)	Puerto Rico (USA), Nairobi (Kenya)	Santa Cruz (Bolivia), Guinea (West Africa), Manila (Philippines)	Buenos Aires (Argentina), Abidjan (Côte d'Ivoire - Western Africa)	Hong Kong, Guinea (West Africa), Bogota (Colombia), Bangkok (Thailand)	United Kingdom, United States

Notes: Shades in the table denote the following:

☐ Responsibility lies with the public sector/government.

☐ Responsibility is shared between the public and private sectors.

☐ Responsibility lies with the private sector but may vary according to the contract agreement.

Source: Idelovitch and Ringskog (1995); Kessides (1995); Israel (1994).

For example, the public water utility/company—Empresa Metropolitana de Obras Sanitarias (EMOS)—in Santiago (Chile) entered into a contract for operation and maintenance of standpipes, meter reading, billing and collection, etc. EMOS encouraged its employees to leave the company and form private firms that can bid for service contracts. As a result of this policy, EMOS has been successful in reducing its own staff and achieving one of the highest staff productivity rates in this sector in Latin America. São Paulo and Rio de Janeiro (Brazil), Bogota (Colombia), Caracas (Venezuela), Santiago (Chile), Buenos Aires (Argentina) and Haiti are some examples from Latin America where components within the solid waste management system—waste collection, transfer and disposal—are handled by private contractors.

In Africa, the practice of contracting out solid waste collection services to the private sector exists in Dar es Salaam (Tanzania) and Accra (Ghana). In both cases, the initiative was taken due to the inability of the city government to deal with the mounting problems of waste collection and the belief that the market would help to overcome this problem. Kassim and Ali (2006) and Kaseva and Mbuligwe (2005) have analysed the role of the private sector in Dar es Salaam. Their study shows a marked improvement in waste collection due to the involvement of the private sector. On the contrary, Obirih-Opareh and Post's study (2002) on the system of solid waste collection in Accra points out that though 'privatisation has benefited consumers in terms of wider coverage, higher frequency, and more reliable services, there are a number of drawbacks, notably worsened labour conditions and increased environmental dangers'.

Attempts to privatise some municipal services in Johannesburg (South Africa) have, however, attracted considerable popular opposition. A plan (namely iGoli 2002) prepared to facilitate the creation of a Unicity provided for a small amount of privatisation as well as management contracts for private companies (including international firms) to operate services such as water and electricity provision. Parnell and Robinson (2006) observe that this initiative led to the emergence of an 'anti privatisation forum, which linked municipal unions, leftist intellectuals and emerging popular movements. This grouping developed a strong critique of the restructuring process, both in terms of the role of private companies in managing council functions and the consequences of amalgamation for employees'.

References

Aijaz, R. (2008). "Form of Urban Local Government in India", *Journal of Asian and African Studies* 43(2): 131-154, USA: Sage Publications Ltd.

———. (2007). "Challenges for Urban Local Governments in India", Asia Research Centre *Working Paper* 19. UK: London School of Economics and Political Science.

Estache, Antonio (ed.) (1995). "Decentralising Infrastructure-Advantages and limitations", *World Bank Discussion Papers* No. 290. Washington, D.C.: The World Bank.

Etten, Joris Van and Leon Van Den Dool (2001). "Building Capacity to Improve Governance", *Habitat Debate* 7(1): 24-25.

Government of NCT of Delhi (2006). "Speech of Sheila Dikshit", Chief Minister of Delhi, National Development Council Meeting, New Delhi. 9 December.

Haque, M. Shamsul (1997). "Local Governance in Developing Nations: Reexamining the Question of Accountability - Editorial introduction", *Regional Development Dialogue* 18(2): iii-xxiii.

Idelovitch, Emanuel and Klas Ringskog (1995). *Private Sector Participation in Water Supply and Sanitation in Latin America*. Washington, D.C.: The World Bank.

Israel, Arturo (1994). "Issues for Infrastructure Management in the 1990s", *World Bank Discussion Papers* No. 171. Washington, D.C.: The World Bank.

Kaseva, Mengiseny E. and Stephen E. Mbuligwe (2005). "Appraisal of Solid Waste Collection following Private Sector Involvement in Dar es Salaam City, Tanzania", *Habitat International* 29(2): 353-366.

Kassim, Salah M. and Mansoor Ali (2006). "Solid Waste Collection by the Private Sector: Households' Perspective – Findings from a Study in Dar es Salaam City, Tanzania", *Habitat International* 30(4): 769-780.

Kessides, Christine (1995). "Institutional Options for the Provision of Infrastructure", *World Bank Discussion Papers* No. 212. Washington, D.C.: The World Bank.

Obirih-Opareh, Nelson and Johan Post (2002). "Quality Assessment of Public and Private Modes of Solid Waste Collection in Accra, Ghana", *Habitat International* 26(1): 95-112.

Parnell, Susan and Jenny Robinson (2006). "Development and Urban Policy: Johannesburg's City Development Strategy", *Urban Studies* 43(2): 337-355.

Schubeler, Peter (1996). "Participation and Partnership in Urban Infrastructure Management", *UNDP/UNCHS (Habitat)/World Bank, Urban Management Programme Paper* No. 19. Washington, D.C.: The World Bank.

Suggestions for further reading

Auclair, Christine and Adrian, Jean-Christophe (1999). "Participatory Urban Decision-making Indicators: An Innovative Approach to Monitoring City Performance", *Habitat Debate* 5 (4).

Baud, I.S.A. and Wit, J. De. (ed.) (2009). *New Forms of Urban Governance in India: Shifts, Models, Networks and Contestations*. New Delhi: Sage Publications.

Cointreau-Levine, Sandra (1994). "Private Sector Participation in Municipal Solid Waste Services in Developing Countries", Volume 1, *The formal Sector, UNDP/UNCHS (Habitat)/World Bank, Urban Management Programme, Paper* No. 13. Washington, D.C.: The World Bank.

Dillinger, William (1994). "Decentralisation and its Implications for Urban Service Delivery", *UNDP/UNCHS (Habitat)/World Bank, Urban Management Programme Paper* No. 16. Washington, D.C.: The World Bank.

Dimitriou, Harry T. (1991). "An Integrated Approach to Urban Infrastructure Development - A Review of the Indonesian Experience", *Cities* 8(3): 193-208.

Expert Group on the Commercialisation of Infrastructure Projects (1996). *The India Infrastructure Report - Policy Imperatives for Growth and Welfare*. New Delhi: Jain Book Agency.

Jha, S.N. and Mathur, P.C. (ed.) (1999). *Decentralisation and Local Politics.* New Delhi: Sage Publications.

Kinuthia-Njenga, Cecilia (1998). "Privatisation of Municipal Services in East Africa", *Habitat Debate* 4(3).

Mahadevia, Darshini (ed.) (2008). *Inside the Transforming Urban Asia – Processes, Policies and Public Actions*. New Delhi: Concept Publishing Company.

Nair, Janaki (2007). *The Promise of the Metropolis: Bangalore's Twentieth Century*. New Delhi: Oxford University Press.

Pani, Narendar, S. Radhakrishna and K.G. Bhat (ed.) (2010). *Bengaluru, Bangalore, Bengaluru – Imaginations and their Times.* New Delhi: Sage India.

Peterson, George E. and Patricia Clarke Annez (2007). *Financing Cities: Fiscal Responsibility and Urban Infrastructure in Brazil, China, India, Poland and South Africa*. New Delhi: Sage India.

Pinto, M.R. (2000). *Metropolitan City Governance in India*. New Delhi: Sage Publications.

Planning Commission. *Eleventh Five Year Plan 2007-12.* New Delhi: Government of India.

Planning Commission (2009). *Delhi Development Report 2009*. New Delhi: Academic Foundation.

Ramachandran, M. (2009). *Urban Renewal: Policy and Response*. New Delhi: Academic Foundation and Skoch Development Foundation.

Ruet, Joel and Lama-Rewal, Stephanie Tawa (ed.) (2009). *Governing India's Metropolises*. Routledge.

Sidabutar, Parulian, Nana Rukmana, Robert Van Der Hoff and Florian Steinberg (1991). "Development of Urban Management Capacities - Training for Integrated Urban Infrastructure Development in Indonesia", *Cities* 8(2): 142-150.

Steinberg, Florian (1991). "Urban Infrastructure Development in Indonesia", *Habitat International* 15(4): 3-26.

Taylor, Paul (1999). "Democratising Cities: Habitat's Global Campaign on Urban Governance", *Habitat Debate* 5(4).

The Times of India (2009a). "MCD hits Government Hurdle on Road to Games Site", 4 April.

———. (2009b). "Power Balance Tilted in Government Favour", 28 October.

———. (2010). "Rate Confusion Comes a Full Circle: Deadlock Continues as City Government told it can't overrule L-G's Objections", 13 November.

UNCHS (2001). "Participatory Urban Action Plans in Somolu, Nigeria, UNCHS (Habitat)", *Best Practices Database*.

———. (1998). "Popular Participation in Local Governance Creates a 'happy place'", *Habitat Debate* 4(4).

Wegelin, Emiel A. (1990). "New Approaches in Urban Services Delivery: A Comparison of Emerging Experience in Selected Asian Countries", *Cities* 7(3): 244-258.

World Bank (2000). "Cities in Transition", *Executive Summary: A Strategic View of Urban and Local Government Issues*", Washington, D.C.: The International Bank for Reconstruction and Development.

———. (1999). *Urban Water Supply and Sanitation*. New Delhi: Allied Publishers.

UNDP (1997). *Governance for Sustainable Human Development: A UNDP Policy Document*. New York: UNDP.